Leadership is a privilege. I  leaders we have the opport an organisation's culture just through creating more genuine connections with our people. Connecting people to a vision takes heart, it takes guts, and is driven by passion. Telling stories that resonate and drive an organisation's purpose is a powerful and important part of a leader's ability to truly engage. Read this book, listen, learn, practise, put yourself out there and practise some more—the people you are leading deserve nothing less.

—Andrew Thorburn, Managing Director and Group Chief Executive Officer of the National Australia Bank Group

An insightful read about the human dimension of leadership. Gabrielle has provided a timely exploration of what it is to be a leader in today's complex world with information overload and the expectations of Generation Y. She peels back the layers of what it is to be an effective leader and provides a practical guide to her readers as to how we can better connect, communicate and engage as leaders.

—Janine Kirk, Chief Executive at The Prince's Charities Australia

Gabrielle Dolan provides brilliant hands-on advice for achieving success in any of the various roles you play, and models that advice in the writing of the book itself: it is a full dose of her authenticity, vulnerability and energy. She makes it real to help us make ourselves more real.

—Marty Linsky, Co-Founder and Principal at Cambridge Leadership Associates

Gabrielle Dolan lays bare the myth that traditional approaches to leadership and antiquated management by hierarchy will survive in the era of Gen Y and Millenial workforces. Authentic leadership and emotional maturity are key success criteria for today's leaders as we confront information challenges and disruptive competitors far greater than anything we could have imagined. In *Ignite*, Gabrielle successfully threads humour and personal perspectives, making this a very accessible and enjoyable guide for any evolving leader.

—Kate Hughes, Chief Risk Officer, Finance and Strategy, Telstra

What I love about Gabrielle is that she keeps it real. Sure she's direct, honest and straight, but she also generates real results with her clients and those she mentors. If you're after another self-help tome that blows smoke up your backside, this book is not for you, but if you're ready to take a look at who you are and what you achieve, Gabrielle has the goods.

—Dan Gregory, CEO at The Impossible Institute, co-author of *Selfish, Scared and Stupid*

Gabrielle's book offers a refreshing and humorous approach to thinking about leadership impact. It is quite literally bursting at the seams with practical information, ideas, stories (of course) and stimulating questions. I hope it 'Ignites' you as it has me!

—Hilary Crowe, Vice President, Group Human Resources, Amcor Ltd, Zurich

Leadership is about self-awareness and having the confidence to be you. If you want to know if you are leading authentically, read this book!

—Layne Beachley, seven-time ASP Women's World Champion Surfer, motivational speaker, entrepreneur and philanthropist

If knowledge is power and wisdom is knowledge applied then *Ignite* is that rare book that helps leaders take an idea and run with it. Packed full of practical truths you can use.

—Matt Church, Founder of Thought Leaders Global, author of *Amplifiers*

IGNITE

IGNITE

REAL LEADERSHIP
REAL TALK
REAL RESULTS

GABRIELLE DOLAN

WILEY

First published in 2015 by John Wiley & Sons Australia, Ltd
42 McDougall St, Milton Qld 4064
Office also in Melbourne

Typeset in 11.5/13.5 pt ITC Garamond Std by Aptara, India

© Gabrielle Dolan Consulting 2015

The moral rights of the author have been asserted

National Library of Australia Cataloguing-in-Publication data:

Author:	Gabrielle Dolan
Title:	Ignite: Real leadership, real talk, real results / Gabrielle Dolan.
ISBN:	9780730322535 (pbk.)
	9780730322542 (ebook)
Subjects:	Leadership
	Communication in management.
	Communication in organizations.
	Executive coaching.
	Executive ability.
Dewey Number:	658.407

Cover design: Wiley

Cover image: © Fourleaflover/iStockphoto.com

Author photograph: Nathan Dyer

10 9 8 7 6 5 4 3 2 1

Disclaimer

The material in this publication is of the nature of general comment only, and does not represent professional advice. It is not intended to provide specific guidance for particular circumstances and it should not be relied on as the basis for any decision to take action or not take action on any matter which it covers. Readers should obtain professional advice where appropriate, before making any such decision. To the maximum extent permitted by law, the author and publisher disclaim all responsibility and liability to any person, arising directly or indirectly from any person taking or not taking action based on the information in this publication.

CONTENTS

ABOUT THE AUTHOR

Gabrielle Dolan launched her own practice in 2013 after successfully co-founding and then building One Thousand & One into Australia's leading storytelling company.

Over the last decade, Gabrielle has worked with thousands of high-profile leaders from around Australia and the world, helping them become more real leaders and communicators. She is a highly sought after international mentor and keynote speaker on storytelling and leadership.

Before running her own company, Gabrielle held various senior leadership roles at the National Australia Bank and was responsible for leading major organisational change.

Gabrielle is the co-author of *Hooked: How Leaders Connect, Engage and Inspire with Storytelling* and co-author of *Eliminate Death by PowerPoint*.

She is a graduate from the Harvard Kennedy School of Executive Education in the Art and Practice of Leadership Development program. Her other academic qualifications include a master's degree in Management and Leadership from Swinburne University and an associate diploma in Education and Training from the University of Melbourne.

In 2015 Gabrielle became an Australian and New Zealand Partner at Thought Leaders Global, where she works with organisations to help them gain a competitive edge through thought leadership. She was also nominated in Telstra's Business Woman of the Year awards.

When she is not working in her practice, she can be found working in her vegetable garden at her 25-acre rural property located on the southern coast of New South Wales. She believes that if there were less manure in business and more manure in vegie gardens, the world would be a better place.

ACKNOWLEDGEMENTS

A book is very rarely a solo effort and this is no exception.

I would firstly like to thank my friend of over 30 years Gail Holstock, who undertook the vast majority of the research for *Ignite*. Her research and suggestions gave weight to my thoughts and concepts and was the catalyst for many inclusions in this book.

A huge thanks to graphic designer extraordinaire Jodie Brennan, who takes my scrappy drawings of models and designs them so they look cool and sleek.

The book was brought up a notch or three by Jo Stewart, who undertook the initial editing process. Her work has helped turn this book into something I am very proud of and I thank her for her tough love.

I would also like to thank Lucy Raymond from Wiley for her ongoing support for my writing and initial guidance when the book was still in its conceptual stage. Thanks also to Ingrid, Alice, Pete and the rest of the Wiley team who provided valuable insights throughout the process.

Thanks to Wiley's editor, Charlotte Duff. Charlotte enhanced the book even further and made the editing process a joy.

A very special thanks goes to Matt Church and Peter Cook of Thought Leaders Global. Both helped with the concept of the book and provided valuable input along the way. They continue to support, challenge and inspire me. They are legends and I am proud to be a Thought Leader Partner alongside them. Thanks for letting me play.

A massive thanks to Michelle Sales who encouraged me to go to Harvard with her for an Adaptive Leadership program. In the days following—between shopping trips and wines in New York—Michelle helped me make sense of many of the Harvard learnings and insights that we have since incorporated into our leadership program for senior women, called The Leadership Connection. This is a program we are both immensely proud to chair.

The book would not be the same if it were not for the people who allowed me to share their stories. I thank you all from the bottom of my heart for being part of this. I would also like to thank the many people that took the time to read the manuscript and provide testimonials.

I also thank the clients who continue to grow with me and support me. Particularly Cindy Batchelor, Natalie Mina, Fiona Robertson, Georgia Russell, Sonia Aplin, Mark LeBusque and Jac Phillips. I love working with you.

A special thanks to Elise Turner, who is firstly my friend and secondly my executive manager. Elise has undertaken, and will continue to undertake, a lot of the marketing and logistics for *Ignite*—and just makes my life easier and work a hell of a lot more fun. Thanks mate!

Finally, a very special thanks to my husband, Steve, and daughters, Alex and Jess. They continue to support and believe in me and always let me blog about them ... granted, they don't normally find out until after it has been published. They allow me to live the dream and they make everything worthwhile. Love you.

And, of course, thank you for reading this book. I hope after reading *Ignite* you will join me in the challenge to get real. The people you lead crave it and deserve it.

INTRODUCTION

The secret of change is to focus all of your energy, not on fighting the old, but on building the new.

—Socrates, Greek philosopher

I entered the workforce in 1985, smack-bang in the middle of the eighties. The eighties were good times. They were fun times. For many reasons, but maybe especially because of the music. I mean, it's pretty hard not to enjoy yourself when your soundtrack includes 'Walking on Sunshine' and 'We Built this City'.

Business was also a good place to be during the eighties because leaders were more real. Long lunches were the norm. Being in the office on Friday afternoon was for 'try-hards'. Life was good. Then something happened in the late eighties…we had a recession. Demand for jobs far outweighed the supply. All of a sudden, the fun stopped.

Everyone was so scared of losing their job they started to work harder and longer. They tried to blend in so they would not get noticed.

As leaders, we enrolled in MBAs, hoping this extra qualification would help us find our next job or secure our current job. In our MBAs, we were taught about SWOT analysis and TOWS analysis, balance sheets and Porter's Five Forces model. We were shown how to measure and capture data, and use data to make business decisions. And we came out the other end a little bit... well, quite frankly—a little bit boring and full of crap.

'If you can't measure it, you can't manage it,' became the mantra in businesses, and a strong focus on data, stats and analysis emerged. This reliance on data was not only how employees and managers alike were measured, but also how we were motivated. The common trajectory went something like this: 'Here is the target, you can do it, this is how we are tracking, try harder, this is the result... oh, and you failed'.

All the data everyone was gathering, combined with the explosion of the internet and search engines such as Google, meant we had more information than we could ever possibly need or want.

At the same time, PowerPoint came along and with it the promise that how we presented would change forever—our presentations would now be interesting and engaging. We could choose how slides transitioned and which sound effects to use—and don't forget how exciting clipart was. With these tools, you could transform any presentation into a masterpiece. And PowerPoint did change the way we presented, but just not as we expected. What PowerPoint (or should I say the poor use of PowerPoint) accomplished was to condemn us to a sort of presentation hell of bullet-point infinity.

Then during 2007 and 2008, the global financial crisis (GFC) hit and job security again became an issue. Considered by some economists to be the worst depression since the Great Depression of the 1930s, the GFC meant we were all scared of what would happen. So we again bunkered down and didn't do too much to attract attention. We certainly didn't do anything to rock the boat—that would be too risky.

But in the business world today, something is happening that means that assumed safe place is actually a risky place to be.

We have a generation of employees who are expecting a lot more from the companies they work for and the leaders they follow. Within five years, generation Y (or the Millennials) will make up the vast majority of the workforce, and they will be the most educated generation in history. The focus of this generation's loyalties has changed, and the expectations they have of their employers and leaders are significantly higher. They want leaders who excite them and ignite them. They want leaders who are real.

The possibility of more money or a promotion does not motivate employees as it once did. This generation wants purpose in their job, and they expect it to be interesting and fun. These expectations are also rippling through the rest of the workforce.

Businesses today are struggling with how to manage this new generation and workforce. But the solutions are available. More than ever, we are looking for leaders who can engage, inspire and ignite this new wave of employees.

The growing expectations of employees are also combined with the exponential growth in technology, social media and access to information. This has resulted in further information overload, making it even harder to get cut-through with your messages.

Organisations invest vast amounts of time and resources into developing strategy and defining corporate culture and values, only to see these efforts fail due to leaders being unable to communicate values in a way that connects and engages with their employees—in a way that is real.

This book is about helping you find the real you. Knowing what you stand for, what you believe in and what you value will help you be your real self and the most authentic leader you can. It will help you to lead with courage and confidence.

Becoming real will not only ignite you but also ignite the people around you.

Read on if you believe in real leadership and real talk for real results.

KNOWING WHAT YOU STAND FOR, WHAT YOU *believe* IN AND WHAT YOU VALUE WILL HELP YOU BE YOUR REAL SELF AND THE MOST AUTHENTIC LEADER YOU CAN. IT WILL HELP YOU TO LEAD WITH COURAGE AND CONFIDENCE.

Chapter 1

The game has changed

The game we are playing has changed. The way we operated in business twenty years ago, even ten years ago, is different from how we operate today. Significant factors have driven a change in the way leaders communicate and inspire, with the ability to engage and influence now being one of the most important skills someone in a position of leadership needs to possess.

Every day, leaders need to communicate. They need to talk about everything from organisational strategy and values to messages of change. They have to deliver tough and unpopular decisions and they have to communicate triumphs and successes. They have to motivate, engage and excite. They have to ignite.

The reality is that this is becoming increasingly difficult, and skills used in the past are fast becoming redundant. Leaders need to not only be aware of this but also understand why this is happening—so they can then do something about it.

This chapter looks at some of the recent shifts that leaders need to comprehend in order to flourish and grow as leaders.

Understanding generation Y

By 2020, generation Y will make up the majority of the workforce. Many senior leaders I work with tell me that one of their biggest challenges is to manage and lead generation Y. But, as John Stuart Mill (an English philosopher and economist) once said, 'That which seems the height of absurdity in one generation, often becomes the height of wisdom in the next'.

Generation Y includes people born between 1980 and 1995 (although some ranges include people born as late as the early 2000s). The label of generation Y followed on from the previous generation's label of generation X, and while this seems to be the label that has stuck, this group is often also referred to as Millennials or the 'dot-com' generation. (If you're wondering why the labelling for generations went from 'baby boomers' to 'X', it's due to Canadian author Douglas Coupland, and his book *Generation X: Tales for an Accelerated Culture*. The book was ironically about a generation that defied labels by stating 'just call us X'.)

Over the past few years, comprehensive studies have shown how generation Y is different from previous generations. For example, Deloitte's third annual Millennial Survey, conducted in 2014, polled nearly 7800 members of generation Y from 28 countries. The findings of this survey outline the significant challenges that business leaders face when trying to meet the expectations of generation Y.

Key findings from the survey showed generation Y valued these features in organisations they worked for:

- Ethical practices—50 per cent of those surveyed indicated that they wanted to work for a business with ethical practices.

- Innovation—78 per cent of respondents said they were influenced by how innovative a company was when making employment decisions. Most said their current employer did not encourage them to think creatively. They believed the biggest barriers to innovation were management attitude (63 per cent), operational structures and procedures (61 per cent), and employee skills, attitudes and (lack of) diversity (39 per cent).

- Nurture of emerging leaders—over 25 per cent of respondents indicated that they were 'asking for a chance' to show their leadership skills. And, 50 per cent believed their organisations could do more to develop future leaders.

- The ability to make a difference—they believed the success of a business should be measured by more than just its financial performance, and argued a focus on improving society was one of the most important things a business should seek to achieve.

- Charitable acts and participation in 'public life'— 63 per cent of respondents indicated that they donated to charities, while 43 per cent actively volunteered or were a member of a community organisation, and 52 per cent had signed petitions.

In 2013, PricewaterhouseCoopers (PwC) in conjunction with the University of Southern California and the London Business School published their results of a two-year global generational study called *PwC's NextGen: A global generational study*. With more than 44 000 people participating, the results are similar to those found by Deloitte, and also offer valuable insights for leaders and organisations keen to understand what makes generation Y tick.

According to the findings from the study, generation Y:

- value work–life balance, with the majority of respondents saying they were 'unwilling to commit to making their work lives an exclusive priority, even with the promise of substantial compensation later on'

- place a high priority on the culture of the workplace they choose, wanting to work in an environment that 'emphasises teamwork and a sense of community'

- value transparency (especially in relation to decisions about their careers, compensation and rewards)

- want to provide input on their work and how it is assigned, and openly seek the support of their supervisors

- expect their contributions to mean they are supported and appreciated, and want to be part of a cohesive team.

PwC highlighted that, while all of the preceding statements are also true of other generations, it's not to the same degree. For example, 41 per cent of generation Y would like to be rewarded or recognised for their work on a monthly basis (if not more frequently), whereas only 30 per cent of other generations ask for this kind of frequency.

Generation Y isn't going away and judging them will not help. We need to understand them, and adjust the way we lead them accordingly, in order to lead organisations that flourish.

They have great expectations

Generation Y wants to be challenged; they want to be inspired and they will not accept the status quo. It's this innate sense of curiosity and their ability to question tradition that has given them the moniker 'generation why'.

With so many options available to this generation, if leaders are not providing a workplace that challenges and inspires them, they will seek to work somewhere that does.

I was recently talking to a member of generation Y called Robert. Robert is about 30 and works for a large corporation. He was sharing with me the experiences of his latest performance development conversation. In the corporation he works for, employees are asked what job they would like to be doing in five years' time. Robert thought this was a stupid question because the job he will most likely be doing in five years' time doesn't even exist yet. This mindset is very common for this generation, and while this kind of thinking may be exciting for them, leading such creative employees, whose working lives seemingly don't have the boundaries we once had in traditional business, can also be very daunting.

This generation has different expectations and beliefs about what they want out of work from their employers. Yes, they want to achieve and be rewarded financially but it is not just about that. They are looking for greater fulfilment, more personal development and opportunities to cultivate a more well-rounded life. More importantly, they genuinely want to make a difference and, therefore, they take corporate responsibility very seriously.

Aaron is an example of this. He is a lawyer who worked for a global consulting firm for five years. The incentive for the long hours that came with the role was the possibility of a very highly paid job. But he told me that he came to realise that nothing about the senior partner's life was attractive to him. Yes, they earned a lot of money but he decided he wanted more than that. He is still a lawyer but now works for a company that has a purpose that he fully believes in.

Companies and leaders need to find ways to meet the demands of this generation's expectations or they will risk losing them.

MEMBERS OF GENERATION Y:

- Have great expectations
- Are loyal
- Want to have fun
- Are smart cookies

They are loyal

Due to their tendency to change companies at a much faster rate than previous generations, generation Y has at times been unfairly labelled as disloyal. However, they are simply responding to the environment they were raised in. Many members of generation Y saw their parents lose their jobs in the recession of the late 1980s and early 1990s after decades of service. After witnessing the fallout from this job loss, they are not inclined to provide the same level of loyalty to companies that their parents did. When their earliest exposure to the business environment taught them that world offers little job security, can you blame them for changing roles more frequently than previous generations?

However, just because they are more likely to change employers (the average employee tenure in 1960 was fifteen years; today it is four), this should not been seen as a sign of disloyalty. Gen Ys are loyal. They are loyal to friends and they are loyal to brands. You only have to be outside an Apple store the day before a new iPhone is released to see evidence of this loyalty in the queues that snake down the street and around the block.

Leaders need to make generation Ys feel valued. They need to be more inclusive and transparent in the way they communicate and lead. They need to provide more regular feedback to this generation than they provided to previous generations. They need to be more real. This generation is screaming out for leaders to be more real—and they are getting a lot of support from the members of other generations, who see the value in people who lead with authenticity and transparency.

So generation Y can be loyal. Leaders and companies just need to work harder to earn their loyalty by offering a combination of tangible, real-time rewards, open lines of communication and transparency. The long, distant promise of promotions and job security does not rate for generation Y.

They want to have fun

Generation Y employees expect to enjoy their job. The thought of staying in a job they hate is absurd to them, and you really can't blame them. A mindset of 'If you're having fun you can't be working' will not serve you well if you are leading this generation.

When it comes to having fun at work, I think we can learn some important lessons from the Danes. Many words exist in one language and not in another language. One such word exists in the Danish language but not in English—'*arbejdsglæde*'. '*Arbejde*' means 'work' and '*glæde*' means 'happiness', so '*arbejdsglæde*' is 'happiness at work'. This word also exists in the other Nordic languages but does not exist in any other language group.

On the flip side, the Japanese have '*karoshi*', a unique word that translates to 'death from overwork'. Not surprisingly, no such word exists in Danish. Nordic workplaces have a strong focus on making their employees happy. Danes expect to enjoy themselves at work, and why shouldn't you too? Your employees are catching on to this train of thought and so have increasing expectations that their time at work should be enjoyable.

GENERATION Y CAN BE *loyal*. LEADERS AND COMPANIES JUST NEED TO WORK HARDER TO EARN THEIR LOYALTY BY OFFERING A COMBINATION OF TANGIBLE, REAL-TIME REWARDS, OPEN LINES OF COMMUNICATION AND *transparency*.

As a leader, you don't have to turn into a stand-up comic, but thinking that you can't have fun at work is misguided and, I would argue, not realistic. This approach normally comes from a leader who is perhaps trying to be the serious leader they think they are expected to be. Being a strict, staid boss is an outdated concept. Being more relaxed and open to the concept of fun is more real and gives you a greater chance of connecting and engaging the hearts and minds of the people that work for you.

They are smart cookies

Generation Y is the most formally educated generation ever. Education rates in Australia have been on the rise for decades and this means much of the power has shifted to employees.

Unlike previous generations, members of generation Y don't feel the need to work in an organisation for years before they ask for a change of role or promotion, or increased work–life balance. They know what they expect and demand these aspects from their first day at work — many will run through their expectations during the interview process. I know of one graduate who had interviews with three of Australia's largest corporations. While these corporations were interviewing him, he was also interviewing them. He received offers from all three but he chose the company that had the greater commitment to volunteering in the community through their skilled volunteer program.

What companies offer employees and how they lead will have a significant impact on not only the retention and attraction of generation Y staff but also how well their employees perform.

This is backed up by further studies. For example, the 2006 McCrindle research paper, *New Generations at Work: Attracting, Recruiting, Retraining and Training*

Generation Y, states: 'The findings are clear: unless their direct supervisors and the leadership hierarchy manage in an inclusive, participative way, and demonstrate people skills and not just technical skills, retention declined'.

The research further stated that, 'Their preferred leadership style is simply one that is more consensus than command, more participative than autocratic, and more flexible and organic than structured and hierarchical'. This means generation Y wants managers who talk openly with them and value their input, and an environment where all staff members are kept in the loop.

Avoiding information fatigue syndrome

In 2010 Eric Schmidt, former CEO of Google, stated, 'There was 5 exabytes of information created between the dawn of civilization through 2003, but that much information is now created every 2 days'. Schmidt's figures have since been questioned (one expert writing in 2011 said a more accurate comparison would be that 23 exabytes of information was recorded and replicated in 2002, and that in 2011 we recorded and transferred that much information every 7 days.) However, the main point remains the same—humans are creating, transferring and storing an incredible amount of information every day.

Information fatigue syndrome (IFS), or information overload, occurs when we are exposed to so much information that our brains simply have trouble keeping up with everything. When the volume of potentially useful and relevant information available exceeds processing capacity, it becomes a hindrance rather than a help—and is when we start suffering from IFS.

Information overload has been around for a while and we are certainly not the only generation to experience it. In fact, in the very first century Seneca said 'distringit librorum multitudo', which means 'the abundance of books is distraction'.

With the ground-breaking invention of the printing press (along with other factors), books started to become more mainstream from the 17th century and this led to concerns. French scholar and critic Adrien Baillet wrote in 1685, 'We have reason to fear that the multitude of books which grows every day in a prodigious fashion will make the following centuries fall into a state as barbarous as that of the centuries that followed the fall of the Roman Empire'.

Today, we are experiencing more information overload than our ancestors ever did. To put things in perspective and gain further information about information overload, go to digitalintelligencetoday.com and search 'information overload'. On the 'fast facts' page, you'll find that information overload can lead to short-term memory loss, greater stress and poor health. You can also find stats such as that, on average, Americans consume 12 hours' worth of information and send 35 texts per day, and spend 28 per cent of their work hours dealing with emails. Information overload can also lead to short-term memory loss.[1]

So what does this all mean for leaders?

Herbert Simon (1916–2001), an American scientist and economist, is most famous for his theory of 'bounded rationality' and its relationship to economic decision-making. In describing his theory, Simon coined the term 'satisficing' — a combination of the words 'satisfy' and 'suffice'.

Simon's theory is based on the premise that people cannot digest or process all the information required to make a decision or take a course of action. He believes that not only are people physically not able to access all the information required but also, even if they could access all the information, they are unable to process it.

---

[1] Yes, that was a deliberate attempt at humour.

Simon labelled this restriction of the mind 'cognitive limits' and it is these limits that mean we seek just enough information to satisfy our needs. For example, when you are looking for accommodation for your next holiday it is almost impossible for you to find out about every form of accommodation available. You may look at three or ten places and then make a choice based on that information you have deemed to be 'enough'.

An overabundance of information actually makes it harder to get people's attention—or, as Simon expressed it, 'A wealth of information creates a poverty of attention'.

In business, we tend to add to this overload of information. We send countless emails when having a conversation with someone would be more effective. We CC and BCC people in on emails constantly and a lot of the times unnecessarily—we do so for our purpose only, not theirs.

We can't stop this avalanche of information but we can make a conscious effort not to contribute to it. We could stop waffling on in meetings and presentations and focus on the key point—how do we get cut-through. Employees are overloaded with information, so leaders need to communicate succinctly and with brevity to cut through this and have impact.

Working with six degrees of separation

No doubt you've heard the term 'six degrees of separation', in common usage following the release of the popular movie of the same title back in 1993. The film was actually adapted from a play that was inspired by the real life story of a conman who convinced a number of people that he was the son of actor Sidney Poitier.

The premise of the six degrees of separation theory is that everyone on the globe is connected to any other person on the globe by a link of no more than six acquaintances. So, in reality, you are no more than six introductions away from the President of the United States, the Queen of England or the Pope.

EMPLOYEES ARE OVERLOADED WITH INFORMATION, SO LEADERS NEED TO COMMUNICATE SUCCINCTLY AND WITH BREVITY TO CUT THROUGH THIS AND HAVE *impact*. BEING REAL AND COMMUNICATING AUTHENTICALLY CAN ALSO HELP YOU GET CUT-THROUGH.

In 2008, researchers at Microsoft announced that this theory was correct. They studied more than 30 billion electronic conversations among 180 million people across the globe and worked out that any two strangers are (on average) distanced by precisely 6.6 degrees of separation.

Some say that this concept was linked to the initial thinking behind social media sites. This may or may not be true but what we do know to be true is that the rise of social media has reduced the degrees of separation even further. In 2011, scientists at Facebook and the University of Milan reported the average number of acquaintances separating any two people in the world was not six but 4.74. The experiment took a month and involved all of Facebook's 721 million users.

Furthermore, a study of 5.3 million Twitter users found that, on average, 50 per cent of people on Twitter are only four steps away from each other while nearly everyone is only five steps away.

LinkedIn is set up on only three degrees of separation, in that when you connect with someone:

1 you already know them

2 you know someone who knows them

3 you know someone who knows someone who knows them.

LinkedIn is not just about the degrees of separation, however; it's also about creating opportunities to connect with other people. At the time of writing this chapter, I had 1204 LinkedIn connections (these are people that I already know); from these connections there are 577 247 people someone I am connected with knows, and more than 12 million people who know someone who knows someone who knows me.

So what do these shrinking degrees of separation have to do with being more real?

Well, besides hearing about six degrees of separation, you may have also heard the phrase 'It's not what you know, it's who you know'. To a certain degree this is correct but now it's not about what you know, and it's not really about who you know—it is about who knows you.

Have you ever had someone come up to you and say 'Hi' in a very familiar way? They clearly know you but you have zero recollection of who they are. They then may pick up on this and say something like, 'We met at the Innovation conference last year'. At that point, you may fake remembering them or apologise, stating that you met so many people at the conference that it is all a blur. The reality is that you may have met hundreds of people at that conference and you may not remember them all, but you do remember some. You remember the ones who had an impact on you. The ones who said or did something that resonated with you or something that was a bit different; the ones you had a conversation with that stood out from the other hundreds of conversations you had. And all because that person or that conversation was probably a lot more real.

The same can be true for you. You may meet someone at an event and six months later you have a need to contact them—perhaps for a job, for advice or to share your new product and services. Because you have met them—perhaps you even swapped business cards at the event—you feel confident that you can contact them directly. However, when you make contact with them, they do not remember you. Yes, you may have met them but if you did not make an impression, they will not remember you.

Dan Gregory, CEO of the Impossible Institute, speaker, author and panellist on the Australian TV show *The Gruen Transfer*, talks about the importance of striving for professional fame. In the book he co-authored with Kieran Flanagan, *Selfish, Scared and Stupid*, he argues that positioning is more important than what you have done, and that the professional fame you build determines your success because, above all else, fame opens doors.

Imagine your busy life. Work is hectic, you have a big presentation on tomorrow and you need to take your kids to hockey practice. In this midst of all this, you get a call from somebody you have never heard of who wants to catch up with you for a coffee to pick your brains about your area of expertise. You may make time, you may not. Now, imagine if Richard Branson rings and wants to pick your brains. I'm figuring the kids are making their own way to hockey practice!

I work with many leaders who, at various stages of their career, have had to reach out to a whole lot of people in their network. I ask them to write down all the people they know in the target audience that they are trying to reach. Then I ask them to highlight the ones who know them. Not just those who have 'met' them but those who know them. Really know them. The people who would stop and say 'hi' and call them by their first name if they passed them on the street. Try this yourself when thinking about the people in your network. Unless you can confidently say that is what would occur, you really don't know them and they really don't know you, regardless of how many times you have met.

Also, you may never have met a person but they could still know you or know of you. And if someone does know you, or know of you, without ever having met you, that is more powerful. I often have clients come to me and give me a name of someone who has referred them to me and I do not know this person at all.

The more real you are, the more likely you will have a greater impact when you meet people, the more they will remember you and know you. The more people who know you, the more people will be talking about you and so the more people will hear about you. Being known by many has a ripple effect and increases your professional fame. Your knowing people does not. So instead of striving to know people you should aim to be known by many people.

BEING KNOWN BY MANY HAS A RIPPLE EFFECT AND *increases* YOUR PROFESSIONAL FAME. YOUR KNOWING PEOPLE DOES NOT.

Three brains are better than one

Educating the mind without educating the heart is no education at all

—Aristotle, Greek philosopher

You may be familiar with the expression, 'Two brains are better than one'? Well, imagine if you had three. The good news is you do. Neuroscientists have discovered that we have three independent brains in our body. One in the head, one in the heart and one in the gut. Each involves complex neural networks, completely independent of each other and with a different purpose and function from the other.

Neurocardiology research by Dr Andrew Armour showed that the heart has a complex neural network containing neurons, motor neurons, sensory neurons, interneurons, neurotransmitters, proteins and support cells. The complexity of this network allows it to qualify as a brain. His research also showed that the heart's neural network allows it to operate completely independently from the brain in the head, and that it can learn, remember, feel and sense.

Further research by neurobiologist Dr Michael Gershon discovered the brain in the gut. His 1998 book *The Second Brain* described the brain in the gut as the 'enteric' brain, consisting of more than 500 million neurons that send and receive nerve signals throughout the torso, the chest and organs. This 'enteric' brain utilises every class of neurotransmitter found in the brain located in our heads and, just like the brain in the heart, it can learn and remember and process information independently.

So while the brains in the heart and the gut may look different to the brain in the head, they are brains none the less.

The impact of this research is significant to all aspects of our life. Our relationships, our health, how we make decisions and how we communicate are all influenced by our three brains. The research has given birth to a whole new focus within leadership development programs, where leading companies are developing leaders in self-awareness so they can lead from the head, heart and gut.

In their book *mBraining*, Grant Soosalu and Marvin Oka explore how the three brains affect leadership behaviour.

Their findings show that each of the brains has three core primary functions.

The heart brain is responsible for:

- *emoting*—processing emotions such as grief, anger, joy and happiness
- *values*—what is important to you and your priorities as well as the relationship between your values and your dreams and aspirations
- *relational affect*—your connection to others and how you feel, such as love or hate, caring or uncaring.

The gut brain is responsible for:

- *core identity*—a deep and visceral sense of self
- *self-preservation*—incorporates self-protection, safety, boundaries, hunger and aversions
- *mobilisation*—focuses on mobility, taking action, having gutsy courage and the will to act.

The head brain is responsible for:

- *cognitive perception*—cognition, perception and pattern recognition
- *thinking*—reasoning, abstraction, analysis and meta-cognition
- *making meaning*—semantic processing, language, narrative and metaphor.

Each of the brains in the head, the heart and the gut is fundamentally different, with different concerns, different competencies and different ways of processing what is going on in the world around us.

Soosalu and Oka explore the significant impact this has on leadership, and especially on decision-making. They believe it is critical for all three forms of intelligence to be accessed when making decisions. Without the head intelligence, the decision will not have been properly worked through; without the heart intelligence, the emotional connection and energy will not be sufficient to care or prioritise the decision; and without the gut intelligence; attention to risk, or even the willpower to act on the decision, will be insufficient. The illustration on page 21 shows how your three brains can interact.

If accessing the wisdom of the three brains is essential for leadership, it should come as no surprise that many leadership programs now focus on the concept of using the head, heart and gut when making decisions.

In their book *The Practice of Adaptive Leadership*, Marty Linksy and Ron Heifetz also emphasise the important role that the head, heart and gut play in leadership. Their mantra is that technical leadership is above the neck (from the head), and adaptive leadership is below the neck (from the heart and gut). In May 2014 I had the great pleasure of spending just over a week with Marty and Ron at the Harvard Kennedy School of Executive Education, where I attended their Adaptive Leadership program.

As a warning to you, my time at Harvard had a profound impact on me. I learnt a tremendous amount about adaptive leadership and experienced much professional and personal growth. The insights I gained from this program have heavily influenced the content of this book so I reference my time at Harvard quite a bit. People who know me personally are sick of me talking about Harvard... not that it stops me!

In the classrooms of Harvard I spent eight intense and long days with sixty-seven fellow students from around the world, all drawn together in a vessel where the heat was deliberately raised in order for us to explore and practise adaptive leadership.

Understanding how to use your three brains to make decisions is critical for leaders, and knowing how to communicate in a way that is directed at the three brains is just as critical. Too often in business the way we communicate is directed only at the brain in the head. Communication around change (regardless if it's major organisational change, a new strategy or even a minor change) is often communicated in a very logical way—this is why we need to change, this is what we are going to do, this is how we are going to do it and this is how we are going to measure it.

When we appeal only to the brain that processes the logic of the change, and do not appeal to the brain that is responsible for values and connection or the brain that is responsible for mobility and action, our chances of actually achieving what we want to achieve are significantly diminished.

The way we describe failure or non-action gives us clues to this. Doubts like 'I know it makes sense but it just does not feel right' are telling us that while the brain in the head has processed it logically, alarm bells are going off in the brain in the gut.

Other statements like, 'He didn't have the guts to do it' or 'His heart just wasn't in it' also point to the critical roles the brains in the heart and gut play when it comes to action and success.

When I work with someone who wants to know if they are a great leader or not, I ask them a simple question: 'When you look over your shoulder is there anyone following you?' To be a leader you need to have followers and to have followers you need to be able to connect, engage and inspire them to come with you. To do this, you need to be able to connect with all three brains and to be more real.

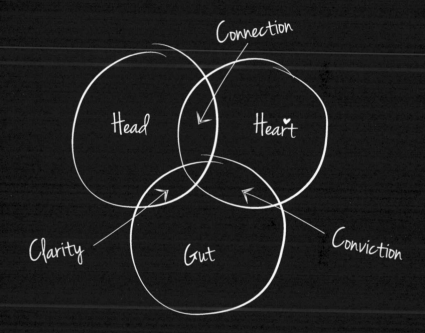

Chapter 2

Finding the real you

A story about a radio interaction between a US naval ship and Canadian authorities off the coast of Newfoundland has been doing the rounds for a while now. Apparently, the conversation went like this.

Americans: Please divert your course 15 degrees to the North to avoid a collision.

Canadians: Recommend you divert YOUR course 15 degrees to the South to avoid a collision.

Americans: This is the Captain of a US Navy ship. I say again, divert YOUR course.

Canadians: No. I say again, you divert YOUR course.

Americans: This is the aircraft carrier USS Lincoln, the second largest ship in the United States' Atlantic fleet. We are accompanied by three destroyers, three cruisers and numerous support vessels. I demand that YOU change your course 15 degrees north, that's one five degrees north, or countermeasures will be undertaken to ensure the safety of this ship.

Canadians: This is a lighthouse. Your call.

Now, there is much debate around whether this event actually ever happened. The US Navy deny it and many believe it is just an urban myth. Regardless, it serves as a great analogy, showing that when we are firm and grounded in our values and beliefs, it is easy to stand tall and hold our position. Granted, being firm and grounded in tonnes of cement like a lighthouse does make it a tad easier.

But very often we come up against the likes of the US Navy ship, just in different guises. People may try telling us we have to divert our course because they are bigger and more important than us. Sometimes people may even revert to threats, or what you perceive as threats, to try to divert you from your course. You will always face pressure to divert from your course, even if it is by the slightest of degrees. This is not to say you cannot be flexible. Of course, you have to be flexible. Life is full of compromises and you have to sway in the wind—but you don't have to uproot your foundations.

True or urban myth, I love the Canadian lighthouse story. I think it highlights that only when we are clear on what we stand for and have a full understanding of our values, can we be strong and stand our ground.

Some call this your true calling or your 'True North'. I first came across the concept of True North after reading Bill George and Peter Sims's book by the same name. The book explains that,

> Just as a compass points toward a magnetic field, your True North pulls you towards the purpose of your leadership. When you follow your internal compass, your leadership will be more real, and while people may not always agree with you people will naturally want to associate with you. Although others may guide or influence you, your truth is derived from your life story and only you can determine what it should be.

One of the benefits of having teenage children is that you keep up to date with modern music. I remember hearing Katy Perry's song 'Roar' for the first time and absolutely loving it. As well as the more obvious reference to 'Eye of the Tiger' from the Rocky films, it also reminded me of Helen Reddy's 'I am Woman'. Because I loved the song so much I had it on high rotation, and I was struck by the opening lyrics and how they reminded me of True North. The lyrics talk about remembering that you have a choice, and you can choose what you stand for. (If you haven't heard the song already go online and search 'Katy Perry Roar' to find the video on YouTube.)

You need to know what you stand for or you will indeed fall for everything.

I am not precious about where I get my inspiration and life lessons from. They can come from urban myths on the internet, professional thought leaders like Bill George and Peter Sims or pop stars—which reminds me of a quote from Ellen DeGeneres related to this. She said, 'Follow your passion. Stay true to yourself. Never follow someone else's path unless you're in the woods and you're lost and you see a path. By all means, you should follow that.' Classic!

Understanding the roles you play

When I was in my twenties I used to work with a man who I really did not like, and I was not alone in disliking this guy. He was rude, difficult to work with and painful to be around. In my opinion, he was overly serious at work and critical. It was like he had divided his life into work and pleasure, and neither of the two areas were allowed to meet. Another woman who I worked with and considered a friend was friends with this guy outside of work. I never quite understood how she could socialise with this complete pain of a person, so I asked her about it. She said that, although he was painful at work, he was actually a really nice guy outside of work. This still didn't really explain his behaviour to me. I just don't buy into that kind of separation, and don't understand why or how someone would do that.

How unbelievably difficult it must be to be a different person at work from the one you are in your personal life. I understand that we may not be completely the same—I know the way I talk to my friends can be different from the way I talk with clients the first time I meet them. However, the difference isn't that marked.

Acting at work not too differently from how you act at home is the essence of being your real self. At Harvard, we explored the concept of the roles we play.

All of us have many roles that make up our whole selves. With each of those roles come different sets of people we have a relationship with. Each relationship brings expectations and loyalties, both from their perspective and yours.

I have the role of mother, because I have two people who expect me to play that role. I have expectations of them but I also have loyalties to deliver on the role I play.

I have the role of wife. I have the role of daughter. I have the role of sister. I have a husband, parents and siblings who all have varying expectations of me, and I have loyalties to them.

I have the role of friend and again have a variety of people who have varying degrees of expectations of me and loyalties to me, as I do of them. The closer the friend, the bigger and deeper the expectations and loyalties are.

I have the role of business owner, which includes the expectations of clients, and I have the role of employer, which again involves people who have expectations and loyalties.

In each of these roles, we behave and act slightly differently. The role I play as a friend is different from the role I play as a daughter. The role I play as a business owner is very different from the role I play as a mother.

Because we have a variety of roles with people who have certain expectations on us in fulfilling those roles, there is always, unfortunately, the opportunity to disappoint. And because we have loyalties to the people we interact with in each of those roles, we will often feel guilt when we do not deliver on those expectations.

Think of each of the roles you play as smaller circles on a bigger circle. Now imagine they are all connected with elastic bands. When you are centred, when you are delivering on all the expectations of the roles you play, everything feels good; the bands are firm but relaxed. As soon as you divert too much focus, energy and time onto one particular role, the end result is normally tension in all the other roles.

You may have experienced this with your friends when suddenly you met a new partner. You started devoting more time, energy and focus on your role as boyfriend or girlfriend, only to cause tension with your role as friend. Your friends may have started to feel a shift in your loyalties and may have been upset by this — even if they were fully understanding and supportive, they likely felt it none the less ... and likely so did you.

You may have experienced this tension when you first got a new job and spent longer at the office trying to make that first good impression or come up to speed with everything. Or perhaps you experienced it during a busy time of the year when you needed to spend more time at work. This likely created tension with the other roles you play because you were less available as a partner or parent. Again, everyone may have been very understanding because they knew the shift was only temporary, but the readjustment of expectations needed to take place.

At the start of 2014 my role as business owner became a lot bigger. My workload was increasing, new clients were knocking on my door and, from a business owner's perspective, this was a great place to be. But I can't deny it put pressure on the other roles I played. I felt the tension in my roles as wife, as mother and as friend. While my husband and close friends were supportive, my two young daughters had greater expectations of me, and so I felt the greater tension.

Of course, tension will always exist between your roles, so you need to manage this. You will not always get the balance right but the more awareness you have of the roles you play, and the expectations and loyalties that go with each role, the better you will be prepared to manage the potential tensions when they arise.

All the roles you play and how you play them is what makes you, you. And as Dr Suess would say, no-one is more 'You-er than You'.

ALL THE *roles* YOU PLAY AND HOW YOU PLAY THEM IS WHAT MAKES YOU, *you*.

Knowing your chimes

I first came across the concept of personal chimes at Harvard. I was intrigued by how much the concept related to a leader's authenticity, and how having a greater understanding of our chimes could help with us being more real. Think of your chimes as your 'hot' buttons—the things that get you fired up, angry, passionate or all three. Some common chimes are diversity, fairness, belonging, authority, inclusion, justice, structure, customer service and process.

Like most things in life, having chimes, especially ones that ring loud, involves pros and cons. Having greater self-awareness, however, can help you embrace your chimes.

Delaying your response when your personal chimes are ringing can be hard, but I am sure you have done it in the past. For example, you have probably been in a situation where you knew someone was deliberately trying to push your chimes. In that situation it was likely easy to respond with 'I know you are doing that deliberately and I am not going to bite'. Or, at least, it might have been possible to think about biting first before you did.

It is important to build this self-awareness because others will probably already know your chimes. They will know your hot buttons and can easily press them for their desired outcome—and their desired outcome may be good for you, or not. A good friend who knows your chimes, for example, may deliberately push them to motivate you to action. A competitive colleague, however, may also know your chimes and deliberately push them to derail you or discredit you.

Throughout my career one of my chimes has been gender diversity. I have always been passionate about this topic—to the point of writing my thesis on the subject in 2002. Early in my career I would pounce on any comment that I deemed to be sexist. This reactive response normally resulted in people not comprehending my message because they were preoccupied with my animated delivery. With maturity I realised the reactive response was not helping my credibility or the gender diversity cause. I still have the chime today and it is still as strong as ever but my response has changed. I still respond but instead of it being reactive it is considered. I find that this response not only helps with getting my message across but also helps with my credibility.

A client of mine, Rebecca, found herself in a leadership team meeting where the issue of increasing the quota of females in senior positions was on the agenda, among other items. Rebecca was the only female on that leadership team, a situation she found herself in often because she worked in the technology sector. When this action item was reached, her manager suggested that they not discuss it as a member of their HR department was not in the room. Rebecca's diversity chimes started ringing—firstly because it seemed this issue was not going to be discussed but secondly because the reason for not discussing it was confirmation from the men around the table that this was not their issue, or a leadership issue, but a HR issue. Rebecca didn't respond instantly, for fear of once again being perceived as the female flying the diversity flag. Instead, she gave herself a few seconds before responding, which was enough time for her response to be considered—even though she agreed there was probably still a lot of emotion in it. Rebecca advised that she was disappointed this topic was dismissed so easily and suggested that HR was not required to address the issue. She emphasised that the leadership team as a group could be doing many things to address the issue.

In the end, time ran out and, because it was late on Friday afternoon, the issue was barely discussed during the meeting. On Monday morning Rebecca asked to see her manager and very calmly suggested that she would be willing to help him with the diversity challenge he and the rest of the team faced. What Rebecca didn't realise was that her response on Friday afternoon had made an impact on her manager—so much that he discussed it with his wife over the weekend. His wife also worked in the corporate world, and she relayed her own stories of the unconscious bias she had faced in her career. She also agreed with Rebecca's suggestion that this was not a HR issue but a leadership issue, and one that he should be addressing.

Within a week, Rebecca's manager had asked her to apply for a role he had not spoken to her about previously—because, previously, he hadn't thought her suitable. It was a significantly more senior role, managing more people and with a bigger budget, and with an attractive salary to match. Rebecca was indeed successful in being offered this role over all the other external and internal candidates. She continues to work with her manager to address the ongoing diversity issues. For Rebecca, being real and true to herself ended up paying off enormously.

Knowing what your chimes are and how to bring them into your role as leader can have a great impact. Reacting when your chimes are ringing always involves an element of risk but, done properly, it can help you become a more authentic leader.

Another example, and one of the more famous incidents of responding to a chime and being more real, comes from Australian politics. In 2010, Julia Gillard became Australia's first female prime minister. From the very early days, there was constant commentary and debate on whether she was being judged harder because she was female. Her clothes, her hairstyle, her choice of partner and her decision not to have children seemed to attract a disproportionate amount of media coverage, especially in comparison to the previous 26 Australian prime ministers.

KNOWING WHAT YOUR CHIMES ARE AND HOW TO BRING THEM INTO YOUR ROLE AS LEADER CAN HAVE A GREAT IMPACT...DONE PROPERLY, IT CAN HELP YOU BECOME A MORE *authentic* LEADER.

Debate still rages in Australia about whether she was treated differently by the electorate because she was a woman, and I don't plan to settle that argument here.[1] For almost two years, however, Gillard deliberately tried to deflect any perceived sexism because she didn't want to play the gender card. But in October 2012 her gender diversity chime was possibly hit once too often and she delivered a fierce and emotionally charged speech directed at the then opposition leader, Tony Abbott. For 15 minutes she accused him of misogyny and sexist behaviour and this speech has now become known as the 'misogyny' speech.

The speech gained a lot of support in Australia and worldwide, as well as some criticism. Some local journalists deemed her speech 'desperate', 'a terrible error' and 'completely over the top'. The *New Yorker*, on the other hand, suggested that President Barack Obama fans might be wishing Obama could take some lessons from Gillard. In the UK, *The Spectator* reported there was 'much to admire' about Gillard.

Regardless of your political view, the nature of the speech had an impact. It was real. I know many who believe it was staged and pre-planned but to me it felt like the real deal. In Gillard's autobiography, *My Story*, she wrote:

> I was fired up. I do not normally think in swear words but my mind was shouting, For fuck's sake, after all the shit I have put up with, now I have to listen to Abbott lecturing me on sexism.

The speech gained worldwide media attention and went viral on social media sites. Days after the video was posted online, it had received over 1.5 million views. To put that number of views into perspective, the next most popular video of an Australian Parliament speech had attracted 14000 views, and was when Gillard shed tears for

---

[1] For the record, I absolutely believe she was treated differently and unfairly because she was a woman.

Queensland flood victims in 2011. At the time of writing, the number of YouTube views of the video was sitting at more than 2.6 million.[2]

Anne Summers, a prominent Australian journalist, wrote an opinion piece that summarised why Gillard's speech had such an impact. According to Summers,

> Here, finally, was a powerful woman speaking out against the sexism and misogyny that so many of us have to deal with. It was something that Julia Gillard has rarely done since she became Prime Minister and certainly not in such personal and impassioned terms. That was what got the response. That was why the speech was so exhilarating — and that was why it has attracted such a huge and impassioned response, here and around the world.

So, regardless of whether you think Gillard's speech was good or bad for her leadership, it had an impact. And it particularly had an impact on those people who felt it came from a place of personal passion and authenticity.

Once you know your chimes, it is easier to take a stand. In Jason Fried and David Heinemeier Hansson's book *Rework*, they talk about the importance of drawing a line in the sand. They suggest:

> As you get going, keep in mind why you're doing what you're doing. Great businesses have a point of view, not just a product and service. You have to believe in something. You need to have a backbone. You need to know what you're willing to fight for. And then you need to show the world.

This is as true for individual leaders as it is for businesses. As a leader, you need to have a point of view; you need to believe in something. You need to be strong and have a backbone and you need to be willing to fight for what you believe in. Not everyone will agree with your point of view.

---

[2]You can view the speech on YouTube — just search for 'Julia Gillard misogyny speech'.

Some people will love it; others will hate it. But you have to be prepared to be strong, just like the Canadian lighthouse. Let other people make their own call but be strong and clear with yours.

Fried and Hansson suggest that 'If no one's upset by what you're saying, you're probably not pushing hard enough. And you're probably boring too.' So be prepared to be real, and to show the real you. Reality may bite but it may also ignite.

Looking at the three 'Yous'

Be yourself; everyone else is already taken

—Oscar Wilde, Irish writer and poet

I want to share with you an experience I had during a workshop that had a profound effect on me. As part of the workshop we were split into smaller teaching groups of twelve. Two students at a time were encouraged to practise a pedagogy (a very cool, academic way of saying 'mode of teaching') that we did not normally use and that would stretch us. Each session went for 20 minutes with a debrief at the end.

One of my fellow students, Helen, wanted to practise the pedagogy of storytelling and started the session with a very personal story of when she was humiliated at school. She told of the lasting impact that this experience had had on her adult life and career choices.

Upon hearing Helen's story, another colleague was so moved that he shared his own story of being humiliated and bullied when he was six, and reiterated that this had also had a large impact on his life. His story was moving and heartfelt and you could see the physical and emotional reaction from the rest of the group. I, with many others in the room, was brought to tears. Everyone was emotionally moved, except one person.

During the debrief following the session, this person said that he did not find his story authentic. Further debriefing uncovered that while he believed the story to be true he did not believe the other person's reason for sharing it. He believed that the other person was using the story so the group would feel sorry for him and accept him. He, therefore, found the story inauthentic because he was challenging the motives behind telling it.

In analysing his reaction it is important to understand what had happened just before the sharing of stories. Just before that session, he had presented along with the man who shared his very personal emotional story. Their presentation was heavily criticised by the group, especially the role this person had played. He was understandably feeling a bit disappointed and maybe even at that stage isolated and annoyed with the group. The very nature of the workshop involved much self-reflection and analysis, and the feedback was often very confronting. He most likely felt he had an ally in his presenting partner. So when he heard him tell his story and saw the group respond so positively to that, he could have felt betrayed by him and suddenly even more isolated from the rest of the group. Hence he challenged his motives. This was analysed again the next day and a whole conversation emerged around authenticity as a leader.

Maybe he was reacting to other things as well. Maybe he's now embarrassed by his response and would act differently today. Who knows? I can't really tell his side of the story in these events. What I can describe is the realisation I came to from his reaction.

Days after, I continued to reflect on this experience because it really concerned me. How could someone so genuinely authentic and real still be perceived in a different way?

And, if that was the case, what was the point? Is my whole message of being 'real' a complete waste of time?

After many discussions over coffee (and some over a wine or three), I decided that maybe the 'real' you was a combination of three 'yous':

- Inner you — what you believe and what you value. This involves all the True North aspects and chimes discussed in this chapter.

- Outer you — the actions and decisions you make. This is the part of you that people can observe. What they see, what they hear and what they feel and experience from you.

- Perceived you — how others see you. You could have complete and total alignment between your inner you and outer you but you are still at the mercy of how others perceive you.

The inner you and outer you is what you have greatest control over but the perceived you is where you can lose that control. So what is the point? What is the point of having your inner you aligned with your outer you if you have no control over how you are perceived? Well, even though I can give you no guarantee, I believe the more aligned with your inner and outer you are, the greater will be your chances that the perceived you will also be aligned. This won't be the case all the time, with all people, but you do have a greater chance that the perceived you will be the real you.

THE 'REAL' YOU IS A COMBINATION OF YOUR:

- Inner you — what you believe and what you value
- Outer you — the actions and decisions you make
- Perceived you — how others see you

Finding your unique self

When my daughters were younger I enrolled them both in karate classes. I strongly believed that having my daughters learn a martial art would be good for them, and that this was a good skill to have. The physical and mental toughness cultivated from martial arts training would be beneficial, as would be the ability to protect themselves. So I enrolled my girls in karate and they both seemed to really enjoy it. Having learnt karate myself for a couple of years, we were able to practise together.

After a year, my eldest daughter, Alex, asked if she could swap karate for ballet. I was a bit reluctant to just allow her to swap so I suggested she stick with karate for a while and promised we would look into ballet later. Perhaps a bit of selfishness was present here in that I saw more value in karate than ballet. Maybe a lot of selfishness here but we persisted for another term, all the time Alex talking more about ballet and looking extremely uninterested in karate. I remember one karate training session vividly. The class was going through all their punches, blocks and kicks, but Alex's kicks did not resemble what anyone else was doing. They were graceful and pretty, strong but in a different way to the powerful karate kicks. After the class I asked her, 'What was going on with your kicks? What type of kicks do you call those?' She replied with, 'They're ballet kicks'. It was then I realised I was fighting a losing battle. I was wasting her time and my money on karate. The next week we enrolled in ballet and jazz. Alex now does ballet three times a week and practises and stretches every day without me ever having to ask her.

Alex is now working towards her strengths and her passion. The energy she shows for dance is 100 times greater than what she ever showed for karate—and that includes when she first started karate and was relatively excited and happy to be doing it.

During my career I've experienced my fair share of performance appraisals that identified my weaknesses and how I could improve them. I remember very early on in my career, in my very first job, my manager advised me during one performance appraisal session that I was not getting paid to be the office clown. While I assured him I was not charging extra for my humour, I did take this advice onboard and made every attempt to 'be more serious'. Of course, this was going against my real self. I can't tell you how many hilarious comments I thought of but did not share. When I was overlooked for a supervisor role for someone older and more serious, yet less experienced, I knew it was time to move on. Working on my perceived weakness was going against my real self and so it would be better for me to work in an organisation that perceived weaknesses as strengths—and appreciated my humour. I now wonder how many people were forced to perfect their karate kicks when all they wanted to do was dance.

I was reminded of this experience when I first came across the concept of 'Your Unique Self' from Matt Church at Thought Leaders Global, and an activity he recommends.

When I first did this activity I found it so liberating. It gave me the confidence and the permission to be my absolute real self. It showed me how I could make any potential weaknesses in my character, style or leadership work for me—and I say 'potential weakness' because I believe all our strengths and weaknesses are on a spectrum. Depending on the situation, they can become either a bigger weakness or bigger strength.

So let me share the process you go through to identify your unique self—and I hope you find it as liberating as I did.

The first thing you need to do is grab a piece of paper and divide it into three columns. At the top of the first column put STATED NEGATIVE. At the top of the middle column put SPUN RESULT. At the top of the last column put POSITIVE OPPOSITE.

Starting in the first column, write down your worst possible traits. These are things your partner or best friend (maybe they are now your ex-partner or ex-best friend) have said to you in the heat of the moment, normally proceeded with something like, 'The problem with you is that you are so damn...'.

When you write these down, they have to hurt. Don't put down anything that you are secretly proud of. For example, when I first did this activity, I started with a stated negative of 'smart-arse'. I get called that a lot but I know I actually wear the label as a badge of honour and a certain amount of pride, so I changed it to 'arrogant smart-arse'.

This is the time to dig deep and be really honest with yourself—you will get nothing out of this activity if you aren't.

So, here are some of my stated negatives:

- hard to please
- arrogant smart-arse
- opinionated
- dismissive (always interrupts)
- judgemental
- impatient.

Now that hurts. I sound like a real bitch.

Once you have five to six stated negatives, move to the last column. This is where the absolute opposites of your stated negatives go. For me, the positive opposites of my stated negatives are shown in the following table.

Stated negatives versus positive opposites

Stated negatives	Spun result	Positive opposites
Hard to please		Easy to please
Arrogant smart-arse		Humble
Opinionated		Considerate
Dismissive (always interrupts)		Good listener
Judgemental		Accepting
Impatient		Patient

The positive opposite is what you have probably been given feedback on during such activities as 360 Degree Feedback and performance appraisals. For example, 'You need to be more patient and humble'.

Once you have stated the positive opposite, use a big red pen to put a cross through the whole lot because you are never going be that person... ever! And the good news is, you don't have to be that person.

You will, of course, no doubt demonstrate those behaviours at times and in certain situations but they do not represent your default position. I know at times I can be very patient (I am a mother, after all) and accepting, and a good listener. But I also know that when I am like this, I am working at it.

To complete the activity, fill out the middle column. This is the spun result of the stated negative. This is where you can pretend you are a spin-doctor for a political candidate. How could you 'spin' your stated negative? For example:

- my 'hard to please' became 'I want people to achieve their full potential'

- arrogant smart-arse became 'witty'

- opinionated became 'strong in my convictions'

- dismissive and always interrupts became 'forward thinker'
- judgemental became 'discerning'
- impatient became 'action orientated'.

The middle column provides some great insights into what could become your signature style or your best self.

If I were described as 'an arrogant smart-arse who is opinionated, dismissive, judgemental, impatient and hard to please', I would be horrified. Yes, I have all those traits but they are me at my absolute worst.

If I were described as 'a humble, considerate, good listener who is accepting, patient and easy to please', I would ask whether they had the right person! I would, however, love to be described as a discerning, action-orientated, witty, forward-thinking person who is focused on helping people reach their full potential.

This activity doesn't give you the green light to completely ignore weaknesses you could work on. For example, interrupting people is an annoying trait and in my line of work as a mentor I know that interrupting does not serve me well and does not allow me to provide the best possible advice and guidance I can, both professionally and personally. So, I have worked on this and have tried to suspend judgement and become an active listener.

WHEN YOU ARE OPERATING WITHIN YOUR BEST SELF, YOU ARE THE REAL *you*.

However, I encourage you to do this activity to see if the process provides any insights into your unique self—because when you are operating within your unique self, you are the real you. Operating as your unique self may not be perfect but doing so will allow you to be your own true self. When people move closer to operating as themselves and as their unique self, they start to be more real. All you need now is the confidence and courage to step into your real self … warts and all.

When I look at myself, warts and all, I take comfort in a quote attributed to Marilyn Monroe (although some debate exists about whether she said it): 'I'm selfish, impatient and a little insecure. I make mistakes, I am out of control and at times hard to handle. But if you can't handle me at my worst, then you sure as hell don't deserve me at my best.'

Chapter 3

Stepping into the real you

*The two most important days in your life are the day
you are born and the day you find out why.*

—Mark Twain, American author

Stepping into the real you takes confidence—and maybe
a healthy dose of ignorance. It may also take competence
but confidence trumps competence all the time. It's natural
for people to misinterpret confidence as competence.
Perhaps because doing so is a judgement call and making
this call is easier—determining a person's competence
usually involves some form of test or observation, and that
takes time. A judgement call on their confidence is often
instantaneous. It may not be accurate but it is a judgement
nonetheless. If you believe someone to be confident, you
will assume they are competent and vice versa. If you sense
a lack of confidence, you will assume a lack of competence.
This may not be fair but it is what people do. So, as
leaders, it is important for us to not only feel confident,
but also aim to project confidence. Obviously, confidence
and competence together is the ultimate goal, but many
leaders have more than enough competence—what they
lack is confidence, and it is this area they need to work on.

Many things can cause a lack of confidence, and I explore a few instances in this chapter.

The confidence muscle

I have always believed that confidence is like a muscle. You need to keep working at it on a regular basis to keep it strong and, if you want to get stronger, you need to lift heavier weights. That's why I love the work of Katty Kay and Claire Shipman. In their book, *The Confidence Code*, they state that confidence is affected by three aspects: our genetics, our environment and our choices.

With genetics, the reality is that some people are born with more confidence than others—and we can't do anything about that. Many use this as a cop-out and they shouldn't, because there are two other aspects of confidence.

CONFIDENCE IS LIKE A *muscle*. YOU NEED TO KEEP WORKING AT IT ON A REGULAR BASIS TO KEEP IT STRONG AND, IF YOU WANT TO GET STRONGER, YOU NEED TO LIFT HEAVIER WEIGHTS.

Environment also plays a part in how confident we are. If you are in an environment that is encouraging and supportive, this will have a positive impact on your confidence. If you are in an environment that is not supportive, where people are always questioning you, this will have a negative impact on your confidence. This environment could be at work and could relate to the culture, your direct leader or your peers. Or this environment could be closer to home—it could relate to your partner, your family and your friends.

Do you have a supportive partner or close friends who encourage you and believe in you? Or are you constantly being undermined and questioned with comments like, 'What are you doing that for?' and 'That's a stupid idea'. We may not always have total control over our environment but most of the time we do have some control, and perhaps we have more control than we think. Most of the time we can choose who we surround ourselves with and who we seek advice from.

The final aspect involves the choices we make, and we all have total control of this. In *The Confidence Code*, Kay and Shipman talk about choice being a muscle, and that the more you use it and test it, the stronger it will become. They also state that women are less likely to exercise the confidence muscle through the choices they make because they are 25 per cent more prone to perfectionism.

Kay and Shipman offer a definition of confidence as 'being prepared to fail'. Anyone who suffers from perfectionism is less likely to have a go at something because the risk of failure (or not getting it perfect) is too great, so they don't exercise that confidence muscle. I love this definition because I hear many of my female clients (and most are very successful women) say that they lack confidence because they often get nervous or anxious. It is worth remembering that confidence is not about never getting nervous or anxious or doubting yourself; it's about feeling those nerves and experiencing that doubt and having a crack anyway.

While I was reading *The Confidence Code*, I went to the gym and had a body scan that measured my weight, height, percentage of body fat and skeletal muscle mass (the muscle that powers movement of the skeleton). During the explanation of the report, the instructor advised that there were many genetic factors that we have no control over (height being the most obvious), but that there are many aspects that we can control through the choices we make (such as diet and exercise).

One of those aspects that we can change through the choices we make is skeletal muscle mass. By increasing the amount of weight work we undertake, our skeletal muscle mass increases, which also makes our bones stronger. This is especially important for women, who are more prone to osteoporosis. I started to feel an analogy coming on—this time between the confidence muscle and the skeletal muscles, and how both are critical for women in making us stronger and protecting us from the eventual falls and knocks we are bound to experience at some stage.

The more we exercise these muscles, the better for us in the short term and the long term, because when we are challenged or experience a downfall, the likelihood of us breaking is reduced. Maybe we won't even break at all, but just pick ourselves up, dust ourselves off and give it another crack.

So, along with the three aspects of confidence are the three areas of focus you can look at to increase your confidence:

- Stop using genetics as an excuse for your lack of confidence. Blaming your parents for everything runs a bit thin after a while. Grow up and step up.

- Start making choices about who you surround yourself with, and make more time for people who have your back and believe in you—both in a personal and professional sense. This does not mean recruiting in your own mould or surrounding yourself with people who only say yes. It is about surrounding yourself with people who believe in you and, because of that, are able to give you constructive feedback that comes from a place of respect and support.

- Make choices that strengthen your confidence muscle by feeling the nerves and doubts about a certain option, and doing it anyway. When it comes to being more real in your leadership role, this could encompass a range of things. Some will be relatively safe while others may carry a bit more risk. The key is to keep challenging yourself and strengthening that confidence muscle.

Strengthening your confidence muscle could include ditching the PowerPoint for your next presentation, making a stand for one of your chimes (refer to chapter 2), being prepared to show vulnerability and emotion at work or just deciding to be more real. The point is to just get that confidence muscle working. As Dale Carnegie says, 'Inaction breeds doubt and fear. Action breeds confidence and courage. If you want to conquer fear, do not sit home and think about it. Go out and get busy.'

Just like exercising your muscles, there is no gain without pain.

Strength in vulnerability

When Alex, my eldest daughter, was nine, I overheard a conversation she was having with a friend's daughter. Alex was explaining to Mia how smart she was and she confirmed this by saying, 'I know I am smart because my mum always says I have an answer for everything'. Mia's mum and I were crying with laughter so much it hurt. Sadly, I had to tell Alex what that saying really meant. Luckily she took it well.

So, as a leader, are you known for having an answer for everything in that bad kind of way? This is not an attribute you want to strive for. Unfortunately, early in our career as we climbed our own specialist technical ladder, having an answer for everything was a good thing and, in most cases, something we were rewarded for. As you move into more senior leadership roles, however, having an answer for everything is no longer something you should be striving for. Unless, of course, your answer is something like, 'That is a very challenging problem but I have every faith in you that you can resolve it. If there is anything I can do to support you, let me know.'

In David Weinberger's book *Too Big to Know*, he explores the explosion of data since the beginning of the digital age, and the impact that this has had on leadership. Turns out (as I cover in chapter 1), this overload of information has made decisiveness difficult. He suggests that, as business becomes more complex and the amount of information leaders have access to continues to grow, the network is what makes the best choices rather than the single leader. In other words, it is unwise for a leader to think they are the smartest person in the room and that they need to make the decisions—because, as Weinberger suggests, the smartest person in the room is the room itself.

According to Marshall Goldsmith's book *What Got You Here Won't Get You There*, 80 per cent of our success in learning from other people is based on how well we listen. So if Charlie Jones was correct when he said, 'Five years from today, you will be the same person that you are today, except for the books you read and the people you meet', as leaders we better get a whole lot better at listening and learning from others.

I believe that the leader who still thinks they need to be the smartest person in the room and have the answer to everything will struggle in this changing world we find ourselves in. Leaders need to embrace vulnerability, and understand that showing vulnerability is not a weakness but a strength...and that can be hard to do. Howard Schultz, the CEO of Starbucks, sums it up when he says, 'The hardest thing about being a leader is demonstrating or showing vulnerability...When the leader demonstrates vulnerability and sensibility and brings people together, the team wins.'

THE LEADER WHO STILL THINKS THEY NEED TO BE THE SMARTEST PERSON IN THE ROOM AND HAVE THE ANSWER TO EVERYTHING WILL STRUGGLE IN THIS CHANGING WORLD WE FIND OURSELVES IN. LEADERS NEED TO *embrace* VULNERABILITY.

Brené Brown is a professor at the University of Houston Graduate College of Social Work. Her book, *Daring Greatly: How the Courage to Be Vulnerable Transforms the Way We Live, Love, Parent, and Lead*, is a *New York Times* number 1 bestseller and was voted by *Fast Company* magazine as one of the top ten business books of 2012. Her 2010 TEDx Houston talk, 'The Power of Vulnerability', is in the top ten of most-viewed TED talks in the world.[1]

Brown believes that vulnerability is 'our most accurate measure of courage' and is about uncertainty, risk and emotional exposure. She believes you can use the same definition for leadership. That is, that leadership is about being able to show up and be seen even when there are no guarantees.

Brown's research busts a few myths about vulnerability that as leaders we should be aware of. Here are two of them that I think are critical.

Myth 1: Vulnerability is a weakness

While we may respect other people who show their vulnerability, we all too often see it as a weakness in ourselves. As Brown says in an interview with *Forbes*

---

[1] To view this talk, go online and search 'Brené Brown vulnerability'.

magazine, vulnerability is 'the last thing I'm willing to show you. In you, it's courage and daring. In me, it's weakness'.

But showing your vulnerability isn't a weak thing to do—it's hard. For Brown, vulnerability is 'about showing up and being seen'. And that's tough. You're worried about what people will think about you, what flaws you'll expose. You're used to covering up these flaws, playing to your strengths, rather than admitting you might need to collaborate with other people to find the answers. As Brown says, 'We end up hustling for our worthiness rather than standing in it'.

However, a growing number of leaders are understanding the strength in vulnerability. And this is a good thing because a significant number of people, especially Gen Ys, are getting tired of leaders who try to cover it up. They are looking for leaders who have the courage to show vulnerability, and have the strength and confidence to say, 'I don't know the answer, what do you think?'

So showing vulnerability is not a sign of weakness; it is, in fact, the opposite—it is the ultimate sign of strength, courage and confidence.

Myth 2: Vulnerability is letting it all hang out

Some leaders shy away from vulnerability because they think it is about letting it all hang out. But it is not about wearing your heart on your sleeve and crying at the drop of a hat. It is also not about over-sharing or purging.

Showing vulnerability requires boundaries and trust. Vulnerability minus boundaries is not vulnerability; in fact, it can lead to distrust and disengagement.

Vulnerability is about sharing our feelings and experiences with people who have earned the right to hear them. Brown believes, 'We need to feel trust to be vulnerable and we need to be vulnerable in order to trust'.

Even with boundaries and trust in place, opening yourself up, showing the real you, along with your vulnerabilities, does open you up to the possibility of being hurt. Perhaps what you have shown will be used against you. The benefits, however, are worth it. As Brown concluded in *Daring Greatly*:

> Without question, putting ourselves out there means there's a far greater risk of feeling hurt. But as I look back on my own life and what Daring Greatly has meant to me, I can honestly say that nothing is as uncomfortable, dangerous, and hurtful as believing that I'm standing on the outside of my life looking in, and wondering what it would be like if I had the courage to show up and let myself be seen.

Ironically, the leaders who have strength and confidence are the ones most prepared to show vulnerability. Think about your own life and what you regret. When I think of the things I love in my life, I know they are in my life because I have dared to go for them. On the other hand, my biggest regrets are when I have stepped away from owning up to what I want or need from others.

Impostor syndrome

Impostor syndrome (also called impostor phenomenon) is where people are unable to internalise their own success. Despite all the evidence of their competence, intellect and accomplishments, they do not believe it themselves.

The term was first coined by psychologists Pauline Rose Clance and Suzanne Imes in their 1978 research. Over five years they studied 150 highly successful professional women across various fields—women who had earned PhDs, who were respected professionals in their fields and who received praise and recognition from peers and authorities.

The study showed that, despite all their outstanding achievements, these women did not experience any internal feeling of success. They put these achievements down to luck and believed themselves to be 'frauds' or 'impostors'.

This initial research focused on women, and further research has been conducted to identify whether men also experience this phenomenon. Through their research and in their clinical experience, Clance and Imes have found that 'the phenomenon occurs with much less frequency in men and that, when it does occur, it is with much less intensity'. A 1984 study that interviewed American psychologists reported that almost 70 per cent of them felt like impostors.

Susan Pinker's book *The Sexual Paradox: Troubled Boys, Gifted Girls and the Real Difference between the Sexes* also explores impostor syndrome. Pinker believes that the syndrome is purely limited to successful women. According to Pinker, successful men never feel like they are frauds.

Men tend to attribute their success to their own internal ability and effort, and attribute failure to external factors. Women, on the other hand, tend to attribute their successes to external factors such as luck or a one-off effort, and internalise their failures.

Impostor syndrome is not about low self-esteem but feelings of self-doubt are common. Chances are you have experienced impostor syndrome at some stage in your career, particularly if you are female. The following sections explore what the syndrome feels like, some of which may be very familiar.

What does it feel like?

Some common signs of impostor syndrome are typified by the following statements.

'I'm such a fraud'

Sufferers of imposter syndrome feel they do not deserve their current success or position, and believe it is only a matter of time before they are found out—that is, before people realise they really do not know what they are doing.

In the Clance and Imes research, many of the women interviewed believed they had obtained their position through an error. Many of the students in the graduate school, for example, believed they were there due to an administrative error. One female professor stated, 'I'm not good enough to be on the faculty here. Some mistake was made in the selection process.'

You may be saying to yourself, 'Well, this research comes from the 1970s and 1980s. Times have changed.' But, believe me, this syndrome is as common as ever and, as mentioned, most especially in women holding senior positions. I have personally felt the effects of this syndrome early on in my career. When I first started my career I was a trainee computer operator and was placed on a six-year development program, as were the other trainee operators. Every year you had to sit both oral and practical exams to progress to the next level. If you failed, you simply stayed on that level for another six or twelve months until you passed the exams. Many operators reached a certain level and did not progress any further, or stayed on the one level for two or three years before progressing.

Every 12 months, I passed the exams and progressed to the next level without fail, passing many of my colleagues along the way. All the time, however, I felt like a fraud. I acknowledged I had good communication skills but to this day I believe I fooled everyone with my technical ability. I found myself constantly looking for ways to remove myself from that career before I was caught out. When I did leave, I told everyone, 'I left before they found out I had no idea what I was talking about'. I think people believed I was joking. I wasn't.

'I'm just lucky'

Another common trait of people who suffer from this syndrome is attributing their success to luck. They feel like they were just in the right place at the right time.

Over the years, I have come to really despise the word 'lucky'—I almost take it as an insult when people call me 'lucky'. Ten years ago, I left the relative comfort and safety of regular fortnightly pay to go out on my own. It was really hard work. I had twelve months where I did not draw an income. Since then, I have had some good years and some bad years. I have always had the option to go back to a nine-to-five corporate gig but I have stayed true to the life I wanted to create. I feel like now I am living the dream that I wanted. I feel absolutely grateful but not lucky. When people say I am lucky, I feel they are not recognising the hard work it took to get here.

'It's not that hard'

Downplaying success is another attribute of impostor syndrome. With comments such as, 'I was just the best of a bad bunch' or 'It wasn't anything; anyone could have done it', the sufferers tend to discount any success they achieve.

In my practice, I have the opportunity to work with some amazingly talented women who are highly successful in their own right, and many have moments of impostor syndrome. Ask yourself whether you have ever used any of the preceding statements, or felt like you didn't deserve the success that has come your way. If you have, chances are you have experienced or are experiencing impostor syndrome. Also think about whether you've ever used such a statement about someone else. Perhaps you've assumed someone didn't deserve to be where they were and hoped they would be found out as a 'fraud' some day. Think about whether your thoughts and assumptions are perpetuating the imposter syndrome in others as well as yourself, and ultimately stopping you from finding and expressing your real you.

What are the consequences?

When an individual is suffering from imposter syndrome, it can cause real problems for them and the company they work for. Some of the consequences can include the individual having the following:

- reluctance to take on new responsibilities, projects or promotions due to fear of failure

- strong risk-aversion due to fear of failure

- inability to celebrate successes or even talk about successes (which can in turn have a negative impact on promotions and other opportunities)

- an abnormal reaction to negative feedback or even constructive criticism (which can in turn lead to unprofessional behaviour)

- increased levels of stress and anxiety due to the constant worry of being found out.

I also believe the syndrome creates another significant consequence that relates to leadership and being real. If you constantly live with the fear that you will be caught out, you will be less likely to stand out or just to be your true, real self.

I went to a Catholic school where wearing a school uniform was compulsory. I can still recall the days when I forgot to wear my blazer and I would do my best to blend in and hide among my classmates at school assembly so I would not be found out.

People who suffer from impostor syndrome spend a lot of time trying to blend in, making sure they don't get found out.

With this weight around their neck, how can they possibly have the courage to make a stand? To be completely real, to allow their chimes and beliefs to guide them, to make a tough decision, to be bold and to go against the flow?

Ironically, the more success sufferers experience the more they feel like a fraud. Meryl Streep, who has received numerous Academy Awards and Golden Globe nominations, has said, 'Why would anyone want to see me again in a movie? And I don't know how to act anyway, so why am I doing this?'

What is the solution?

Curing imposter syndrome has no easy answer, but you do have some options to help you deal with the issues:

- *Awareness*—like most things, you first need awareness to make a change. You need to be mindful of the initial and any ongoing thoughts you have. Awareness can often be hard, though, because the feelings are so real. When I look back on my early career, I still find it hard to accept that I had impostor syndrome. If I am completely honest, I still don't genuinely believe I did. I still find it easier to believe my technical skill did not warrant my quick rise through the ranks, and that this success was purely because I was a good communicator and was well liked. I believe this even though I know logically that would never have been enough to warrant my promotions.

- *Support*—it is really important to surround yourself with people who support you. Many highly successful people have support mechanisms in the form of coaches and mentors. If you don't have a professional mentor or coach, at least speak to a good friend or trusted adviser about your feelings.

- *Reframe*—once we are aware and have support, could the solution be as simple as reframing our thoughts and the stories we tell ourselves? While it may not be simple, I believe this reframing can be very powerful.

If Pinker is correct and impostor syndrome is only experienced by highly successful women, then if you are experiencing these feelings, by definition you are a highly successful woman.[2] Could it be a matter of reframing your thoughts? So when you catch yourself discounting success or responding with, 'I'm just lucky' or 'I was in the right place at the right time: anyone could have done it' or when you catch yourself feeling like a fake, instead of labelling yourself a 'fraud', could you reframe the situation and label yourself a 'genius' or 'legend'?

Think about it. You are only feeling these thoughts because you are highly successful. If you weren't, you would not be feeling them.

Logically this makes sense but, of course, changing the stories we tell ourselves is a lot easier said than done. However, it is definitely worth the effort.

Natasha Pincus created and directed the music video clip of Gotye's 'Somebody that I used to know'. This video clip is one of the most viewed video clips in history and has won multiple awards around the world. After the success of the video many people claimed Natasha was a 'genius'. It got her thinking about this—to the point that she wrote a book titled *I Am Not a GENIUS and So Are You*. I had the pleasure of seeing Natasha speak in 2014 and was inspired by her message. She believes that anyone can be a genius but we have to believe it. Believing you are a genius makes you more creative, more empathetic and more productive.

---

[2]If you are male and feel you also suffer from imposter syndrome, go with the Clance and Imes research, which found that the phenomenon does occur in men just with much less frequency and intensity.

You dare more, believe more and commit more. For Natasha 'it means accepting that Genius is a label that can't be given to you by anyone but yourself'. But only 'when you get out of your own way'.

BELIEVING YOU ARE A GENIUS MAKES YOU MORE CREATIVE, MORE EMPATHETIC AND MORE PRODUCTIVE. YOU *dare* MORE, BELIEVE MORE AND COMMIT MORE.

To keep impostor syndrome at bay, maybe we just need to replace our thoughts of 'fraud' with 'genius'. I am a true believer that our thoughts become our words, our words become our actions, our actions become our habits, our habits become our character and our character becomes our destiny.

Imagine if every time you thought you were a fraud, you replaced that thought with genius. Little by little the fraud label you place on yourself can be replaced with the label of genius. The thought of genius may even become so strong at times that you will (because you can't help yourself) proclaim out loud 'I am a genius'.[3] Even if no-one is around to hear it, I encourage you to speak it.

Of course, you need to be careful how you say this. You don't want to tip the scales too much and go from impostor syndrome to the Dunning-Kruger effect. David Dunning and Justin Kruger of Cornell University (in a 1999 study) found that some individuals rate their abilities much higher than the actual reality. In essence, this is the complete opposite of impostor syndrome. Their research was inspired by a bank robber who covered his face with lemon juice

---

[3]Or is that just me that happens to?

believing that, because lemon juice was used as invisible ink, it would make his face invisible on security cameras. I am sure you know people who are like this. Maybe they don't cover their face with lemon juice thinking they will become invisible, but they have an over-inflated sense of their competence—a sense that does not match reality. They can be extremely frustrating and dangerous.

Shakespeare alluded to this in *As You Like It* when he said, 'The foole doth thinke he is wise, but the wiseman knows himselfe to be a foole'. Now that is genius!

Be careful who you take advice from

To be yourself in a world that is constantly trying to make you something else is the greatest accomplishment.

—Ralph Waldo Emerson, American lecturer and writer

When it comes to courage and confidence, you need to be careful who you listen to. Earlier in this chapter, I discussed how important your environment and who you surround yourself with is, but sometimes the voices we are listening to are the ones in our head.

Often the battle of the voices in our head is a good thing. They can sometimes stop us from making a mistake or keep us away from danger. Other times they stop us from taking on a challenge because they provide a very convenient excuse or logical reason not to. However, distinguishing between a reason and excuse can be difficult.

At Harvard we were often asked a simple question when making a statement or contributing to a class discussion, and that was: 'Is that the truth or is that a convenient story you are telling yourself?' This question was unbelievably confronting but it did make you question the assumptions in your head.

I have found this to be a very powerful question to ask of myself and the leaders I work with. When I facilitate my storytelling workshops, I often get some leaders saying something like, 'I have to present to the Board but could never tell a story because they would not relate'. Really? I respond with, 'Is that the truth or is that just a convenient story you are telling yourself?' Because the most likely truth is that they don't have the confidence to share a personal story with the Board.

When you are about to take a risk or challenge yourself, you will always have that voice in your head explaining to you why it is not a good idea, and that voice can be persuasive.

That voice may say something like this:

- *'Don't talk about your faith at work, you will put people off.'*

- *'Don't share a personal story of vulnerability, it will show weakness.'*

- *'Don't talk about gender diversity; it will damage your career.'*

- *'You have to use PowerPoint; you will look unprofessional if you don't.'*

Make the conscious choice to ignore that negative voice in your head that holds you back, and reap the benefits that come from stepping forward and being real.

Say it as it is

My friend Wendy is a financial planner and she spends a lot time at conferences watching people present. These experiences led her to ask me to include a section in this book on avoiding corporate jargon and, instead, 'saying it like it is'. So here it is.

About ten years ago, a colleague gave me a copy of Don Watson's *Dictionary of Weasel Words* as a parting gift. Was this a subtle hint to change my communication style? Anyway, 'weasel words' is a term used to describe words that have no substance or have lost all meaning. The term originates from a widespread belief that weasels suck the contents from bird's eggs, leaving only the empty shell. (Although this is a widespread belief, doubt exists as to whether weasels actually do suck the contents from the eggs. Regardless, the term has stuck.)

In the belief that weasels suck the contents out of eggs, 'weasel words' is used to describe words or statements that have had the life sucked out of them.

Weasel words are also more commonly known as 'management speak' or 'political speak'. That is, the art of talking without actually saying anything. The adoption of such language could be due to the fear of being wrong or the fear of making a commitment or the fear of delivering bad news. Regardless of the reason, people who hide behind 'management speak' or 'political speak' or 'weasel words' are simply not prepared to say it as it is.

The business world and the political world are rife with examples of this. Take this edited extract of an exchange between journalists and Australia's then-immigration minister Scott Morrison, who provided a 'doorstop' press conference in June 2014:

Q: Minister, is there a boat in trouble off Christmas Island?

A: It is our standard practice as you know, under Operation Sovereign Borders, to report on any significant events regarding maritime operations at sea, particularly where there are safety of life at sea issues associated, and I am advised I have no such reports to provide.

Q: Is there a boat?

A: Well, I have answered the question.

Q: ...So are you saying that boats are not leaving [for Australia]?

A: We are always ready for boats that may arrive and we always anticipate that they may seek to come and we are always ready. We are ready today, we were ready yesterday and we will be ready tomorrow and the government's policies will continue to prevail.

Q: So Mr Morrison, you are not even going to confirm there is a boat, you are not going to say what is happening if people are in the water? Their boat is leaking, we are told—leaking oil—and you are not going to say anything about that situation?

A: What I have said is that it is our practice to report on significant events at sea, particularly when they involve safety of life at sea. Now there is no such report for me to provide to you today. If there was a significant event happening then I would be reporting on it.

Q: So what does that mean?

A: You are a bright journalist. I'm sure you can work it out.

Q: No, we are asking you, Sir. You are the minister.

A: And I have given you my response.

Q: So could you clarify, Sir, for us—at what point does an event become a significant event involving a boat on the water?

A: When you see me here standing and reporting on it.

Q: And you are standing here reporting.

A: I am not. I am saying there is no such report for me to provide to you today. There is, therefore, no significant event for me to report at sea.

Q: Are you saying that it could be a hoax that people are saying they are in trouble?

A: I am not saying anything of that at all. I am not confirming any of these matters. This should come as no surprise to you. This has been our practice now for the entire period of this operation. This is another day at the office for Operation Sovereign Borders.

Another day indeed, and another day of being unprepared to say it as it is. Although you can't blame Morrison alone—apparently his department employs more than ninety-five communications staff and spin doctors, at a cost of more than $8 million a year.

Besides avoiding weasel words, if you want to be more real you should also try to use fewer acronyms, less jargon and fewer clichés. Of course, we all do use these from time to time, but make sure when you communicate you do so as little as possible and instead include more of just saying it as it is. Keep it real.

Acronyms

Acronyms (or acronyms and initialisms, to get technical) can be handy when every single person you are talking to understands what they mean. Sadly, this situation is often assumed and can be the furthest from reality.

I can recall a time when I was mainframe computer operator. One of the fans in the IBM processor had broken and I needed to order a new one. I looked up the IBM parts directory for 'fan' but couldn't find it listed under 'f'. I ended up calling them directly to be advised I would find the part number for the fan under 'A' because it is called an AMD ... an air movement device. Really? So, yes, IBM does have a TLA[4] for a FAN and it is an AMD.

When you think about it, acronyms are used as a kind of shorthand. They usually take less time to write and less time to say (although not always!). This is fine for the person writing or speaking. But the person listening or reading has to do all the work to convert the acronym into the full name. Even then, they sometimes don't understand what that means.

---

[4] Three letter acronym.

SAY IT AS IT IS:
- Avoid acronyms
- Get rid of clichés and management speak
- Use analogies and metaphors carefully

A classic example of this is CVP or EVP, which are acronyms for customer value proposition or employee value proposition. As in, 'We need greater clarity on our EVP' or 'We need to ensure that this is aligned to our EVP'. The process in the receiver's heads is likely, 'EVP? EVP? What is that? Ah, yes. It is employee value proposition. I wonder what that really means. I think it means what we offer to our employees that they value. I think? Why can't they just say that? Sorry, what were you saying?'

I know I am guilty of using acronyms at times but I try to use them less and less. Because, when you think about it, if using acronyms makes it easier for you but harder for others, doesn't that just make you lazy when you use them? Or, perhaps worse, even selfish?

Clichés and management speak

I am so clever that sometimes I don't understand a single word of what I am saying.

—Oscar Wilde, Irish writer and poet

Using a lot of clichés and management speak is dangerous. Using this type of language assumes that everyone understands what these terms mean, and that is a flawed assumption. For every person who knows exactly what the cliché or management speak term means, there is likely at least one person who has no idea but is too afraid to ask, and another who has the incorrect interpretation.

Even more concerning, sometimes the person using the cliché or management speak does not know themselves what it fully means.

For example, here are three terms that particularly annoy me:

- *Step change*—as in, 'The current way we are doing things is not working; we need a step change'. I think what this means is that we need to step up a bit or change the pace. To move from a waltz to a tango maybe? I don't really know what it means. I hear it a lot and have now resorted to asking people what they mean. I often get very vague responses about 'changing pace'. Is it just me, or could we not just say 'do things differently'?

- *Executional excellence* or *operational excellence*—I was working with a leader once who used to use this phrase a lot—to the point it was one of their company values. I would hear him and his team use the term in most of their communications to employees. One day, I challenged this leader, saying that I was not sure if people actually knew what it meant and, in fact, I was not even sure if my interpretation of what it meant was correct. He attempted to explain it to me and after a few tries he said, 'What it basically means is that when we say we are going to do something, let's make sure we do it right'. Now, do you not find that more engaging, inspiring and memorable than 'executional excellence'?

- *Close of play*—as in 'I need those documents by close of play'. This confusing term is used to replace the very non-confusing term 'end of the day'. I think this an attempt to bring in a sporting cliché but (outside of cricket) I don't hear too many people use 'close of play' in regards to a sporting event.

The other reason you should avoid clichés and management speak is that they get little cut-through.[5] This is mainly due

---

[5] I think 'cut-through' could even be considered management speak. I never said I was not guilty or that breaking the habit was easy.

to the fact that they very quickly become overused as more and more people in the organisation start repeating them. Like clichés, other words can become the flavour of the month. Words such as strategy, journey, moving forward, narrative, leverage, deliverables and…I am sure you can add many more to this list. This has even started to occur in the Australian Football League with the word 'structure'. Footballers being interviewed after games can now be heard saying, 'Our problem was we did not adhere to our structures' or 'Our structure was solid, which helped with overall play'.

Once these terms become overused they start to lose their impact.

Don Watson has a website[6] that provides many sad but hilarious examples of not saying it as it is. Take the following, for example, that was from a job advertisement for a 'Citizen Services Ambassador' at Births, Deaths and Marriages Victoria.

Citizen Experience Portfolio

The Citizen Experience Portfolio has an intimate knowledge of citizen expectations and emergent trends and strategically defines and navigates BDM's service delivery model to ensure a relevant and sustainable citizen-centric offering. The Portfolio is comprised of the Citizen Service and Citizen Experience Development Teams and has responsibility for the development, implementation and evaluation of services that place the expectations and needs of citizens at the core.

The Portfolio initiates and enables the collaborative exploration and dynamic adaptation of BDM's citizen-centric service delivery model and citizen value proposition.

The Citizen Experience Development Team is responsible for the development and implementation of business transformation and service development initiatives and

---

[6]Go to www.weaselwords.com.au.

accompanying processes and tools. This Team also leads the exploration, analysis and development of citizen-centric discretionary services.

The job being advertised was actually a customer service and administrative role.

Let's look at CVP or customer value proposition again. When you hear that acronym or phrase, do you have any emotional connection to it? Does it excite you? Probably not or maybe only a little.

On the other hand, let me share with you an experience I had recently on a family holiday to Paris. While in this amazing city, I organised a private walking tour for my family so we could discover some local cafés, bakeries and other specialty shops that are off the tourist track. Our guide advised us of a beautiful phrase the French have: *ça vaut le déplacement* which means 'it's worth the trip'.

She was using it to describe the specialty baker known for making the best croissants in Paris. Our guide advised that no matter where you are in Paris, these croissants are worth the trip—we had, in fact, crossed the Seine for them.

My daughter Alex has coeliac disease, so at the time had not had a croissant since her diagnosis seven years before. We had found out that the French process flour differently, which means their flour contains very little gluten, and considering croissants are mainly butter, the croissants were almost (but not quite) gluten-free. We had one very excited daughter on our hands.

Alex's first croissant in seven years deserved to be the best and it certainly was '*ça vaut le déplacement*'.

This beautiful phrase got me thinking of customer value proposition. Imagine if instead of talking about CVP, we shared this story and then asked of our people 'What are we doing, or what can we do, that our customers will cross the river for? That is, what will make them go out of their way to deal with us? So that they will do anything to work with us and only us?'

I suggest we start replacing phrases that have little impact and emotional connection with questions like, 'Is it worth the trip?' For this to work, though, it needs to be communicated via the story. Otherwise, 'Is it worth the trip?' on its own will just end up being another meaningless phrase.

So instead of asking, 'What is our CVP?' ask 'Is it worth the trip?' or '*ça vaut le déplacement*'? But please, please do not reduce this to IIWTT or CVLD.

Analogies and metaphors

Analogies and metaphors can very useful when attempting to explain something. Teachers, for example, use them often in the classroom to help their students understand concepts. Leaders can also use analogies and metaphors, but they need to be aware that they do have their limitations. They can help people understand a concept but not necessarily inspire and engage them.

Sporting analogies in particular should be avoided. Business is not a game of two halves and no-one wins the premiership at the end of the season.

Ensure your analogies will connect with everyone in your audience and keep in mind that if you have to explain an analogy, it's a poor analogy.

Weasel words, acronyms and corporate jargon are not new, and they have always been annoying for the listener. Once I tried to get through a day without using any acronyms or corporate jargon—it was hard and I failed. So I am not suggesting we need to stop using them all together but if leaders want to be more real and to engage better, the less we use of them the better.

Level up

I am a huge fan of J.K. Rowling and besides loving the Harry Potter series I also love her attitude to life. Rowling believes that, 'It is impossible to live without failing at something, unless you live so cautiously that you might as well not have lived at all—in which case, you fail by default'.

I was introduced to the concept of 'levelling up' by the amazing Matt Church and I found it an extremely useful tool in providing the courage and confidence to give something a crack, such as stepping into the real you. Matt talks about vibrating up a level and I prefer the concept of that over the much-used term 'step up'. 'Vibrate up' has a more gradual feel to—it's about making small changes to vibrate up a level. Then, once you are at that level, that becomes your new constant, which allows you to then vibrate up another level.

The first part of the levelling up activity is to choose your challenge. What is it that you want to level up to? For example, when I did this my challenge was to grow my business. But I have done this many times with many clients and their challenges have all varied—from speaking up more to seeking an executive role or losing ten kilograms. Your challenge may be to increase your leadership presence, or it may be a specific aspect of that such as bringing more of your true self to work, becoming a better presenter, becoming a more active listener or increasing your presence on social media. One challenge you could work on is levelling up to be a more inspiring leader and communicator.

Whatever your challenge is, write it in a circle in the middle of a piece of A4 paper. Once you have your levelling up challenge identified, in the top left quadrant of the paper write down all the non-negotiables involved if you were to achieve this challenge. These are normally based around your values.

As I said, when I first did this activity I did it around my challenge to actively grow my business. My daughters, Jess and Alex, were ten and thirteen respectively, and, as a working parent, I was juggling many demands. I recorded my non-negotiables as:

- still spending school holidays at our rural property
- always having time to exercise with my friends
- maintaining my current work–life balance — still enjoying time with my kids, my husband and my friends
- never taking work for the sake of it when I didn't think I could add value.

Then in the bottom left quadrant of the paper, record all the things you will lose if you level up to this challenge.

For me, I listed all the things I assumed I would lose if I actively grew my practice, as follows:

- sleep-ins
- Facebook time
- excuses
- wasted time
- clients I didn't enjoy working with
- my mortgage.

What I love about this activity is that you, and only you, decide what you record here. When I started to write down the things I would lose, I naturally started with the negative things, because when we talk about loss it has negative connotations. However, once I moved past the sleep-ins and being able to waste time on Facebook, I ran out of negatives. I was about to write work–life balance and time to exercise but I reminded myself that these were on my non-negotiable list, which meant I wasn't going to lose them at all. Then I started thinking of other things I would lose and then they became positive ones.

The important thing to note here is that what you record and what you believe you will lose will either support you in your levelling up efforts or sabotage them.

If your list is predominately negative, have a go at thinking of things you will lose that are positive.

Once you have recorded all the things you will lose, move to the top right quadrant and record all the things you should gain if you level up. What will you get by doing this? For me it was:

- financial security
- financial freedom
- sense of accomplishment
- freedom to choose (not only for me but for my family)
- more opportunities
- sense of fulfilment
- complete control of who I work with.

Again you get to choose what you record here and what you believe will either support or sabotage you. If you truly believe these gains are possible, they are more likely to happen. I am a massive fan of positive thinking or, as Matt Church calls it, positive delusion. For example, when I go on a run, I tell myself that I don't stop on runs. I come to a big hill and my positive delusion kicks in and all my mental energy gets me up that hill without stopping. Now I must admit that this does not work 100 per cent of the time — there have been occasions when I have stopped — but it hurts me to even put that in writing because it is going against my positive delusion mindset.

I work with a lot of clients who come to me saying, 'I hate public speaking and I am no good at'. And guess what?

They hate public speaking and they are no good at it. How can you be a good public speaker if you hate it and you think you are no good at it? What would your mindset be like when you had to speak in public? What would your body language portray? Yes, you may need some skill development to address this situation, but you also need a bit of positive delusion.

IF YOU TRULY BELIEVE THESE GAINS ARE *possible*, THEY ARE MORE LIKELY TO HAPPEN.

The final quadrant you need to complete is the bottom right corner. This is where you reflect on your non-negotiables, and compare what you will lose with what you will gain and decide what you know to be true. For me, I wrote: 'Just do it'. I then added the following:

- the non-negotiables are not an excuse
- my family will be better for it
- I will be better for it.

It is amazing what can happen or what you can make happen after completing this activity. I started training for a half marathon with two of my closest friends. We spent a lot more time exercising together and completed the half marathon together.

I also made slight changes to how I structured my day, including changing when I enjoyed my first morning coffee—instead of having it as soon as the kids left for school, I started to have it while I sat down with my youngest daughter so we had breakfast together.

I started owning my position more. Once I made the decision to level up, I just assumed the position of a successful business owner. Outwardly nothing changed; it was just a slight mindset shift in me.

I gave myself more of a break. I went hard but was more relaxed about it. I have always been a fan of stopping and smelling the roses but, again, I just did this more.

I don't know whether it was coincidental but life just seemed to get a whole lot better. My sales escalated and more and more amazing opportunities came my way. For example, I was asked to run a storytelling workshop in London for the International Committee of the Red Cross. I did this and combined it with a family skiing holiday — so suddenly the kids were really excited that Mum had to travel a bit with work.

My husband (who had become increasingly disengaged from his work after spending 26 years in the corporate world) now had the freedom to do what he wanted to do, which was to become his own boss and work with his hands in the building and construction industry.

I recruited two of my best mates (and running buddies) to work for me. So now I get to run and discuss work at the same time — and have a fun Christmas party.

It is amazing what you can do when you combine your non-negotiables with some positive delusion … Genius can happen. You can change your world and possibly the world of the people around you.

Chapter 4
Communicating the real you

The way we tend to communicate and engage our employees is not working and needs to change. The mindset and approach to communication continually evolves and we can't afford to stop this process now. The trend towards such change is driven by the rise and ubiquity of social media, the disruption of conventional 'top–down' approaches to communication and the realisation that we need to engage people in the 'why' and not just the 'what' in our communication. In other words, we need to engage all three brains (refer to chapter 1) and we need to inspire people.

However, too many organisations and leaders still have a cascade mindset to communication, with a focus on the 'what'. This top–down, one-way approach to communication often results in leaders communicating through obligation, with an attitude of just passing information on. This happens because they have not connected to the messages themselves, so it's little wonder they pass on the information in a similar vein.

This approach just adds to the information overload that your employees are already dealing with, and means they either ignore the message, don't understand the message, don't care about the message or feel completely overwhelmed by it.

What organisations and leaders need to do is move to a focus on the 'why' instead of the 'what'. Organisations need to have a clear compelling 'why', and sell the 'why' as opposed to just the 'what' and 'how'. Simon Sinek, author of *Start with Why: How Great Leaders Inspire Everyone to Take Action*, explains how this works—and the power that comes from it. Sinek states that people don't buy what you do; they buy 'why' you do it. And leaders who start with the 'why' have the ability to inspire others around them.

When organisations start with the 'why', and empower leaders to communicate the 'why' in a way that is personal to them, they will have a more engaged workforce.

One aspect of authentic leadership is being able to make tough and unpopular decisions. Once a tough and unpopular decision has been made, leaders then have an obligation to ensure the people not only understand the reason for the decision but are also engaged in the conversation about it.

Engagement, however, is easier said than done. Organisations that conduct employee opinion surveys will testify that, when looking to see how they have fared, the measure leaders look for first is the employee engagement score. It is also one of the hardest measures to shift.

I was reminded of this in 2014 when I visited Boston in the United States for the first time. I arrived a few days before I commenced my Harvard program and, being a tourist, I took part in a sightseeing tour and went along to a Boston Tea Party re-enactment—which included character actors and lots of crowd participation. This would not normally be my cup of tea (pardon the pun) but it was quite educational. I had heard about the Boston Tea Party before but had never really known the details, nor the significance, of the event.

If you don't know the story, here it is at a very macro level. Mother England had imposed a high tax on any tea exported to her colonies (America being one such colony). Many Bostonians were angry about these high taxes, claiming they were a violation of the English idea of 'no taxation without representation'. In December 1773, three ships from England arrived in Boston Harbour with tonnes of tea. Boston refused to unload the tea in protest about the high taxes. The Crown ordered the tea to be unloaded from the ships. Led by Samuel Adams, a group of protesters boarded the three ships and threw all the tea into the water. England reacted by closing down the port of Boston, crippling the city over night. They also despatched over 4000 of its army (known as the 'Red Coats') to Boston.

WHEN ORGANISATIONS START WITH THE 'WHY', AND EMPOWER LEADERS TO COMMUNICATE THE 'WHY' IN A WAY THAT IS PERSONAL TO THEM, THEY WILL HAVE A MORE *engaged* WORKFORCE.

Sixteen months later, the Red Coats came to arrest Adams, and this resulted in the Battle of Lexington, which was the start of the American Revolution. On 4 July the following year, America declared independence from British rule.

Back in my hotel room after the educational tour of Boston, I continued my pre-reading for the Harvard program. Much of this pre-reading focused on defining leadership, with a common consensus that leadership consists of providing a vision and then taking action to realise that vision. And that leadership is also about being prepared to take an unpopular stand but, once that stand is made, the leader has an obligation not only to explain it to the people but also to win their support and approval.

When I look at what Samuel Adams did, I think he ticked all those boxes:

- He had a vision of 'no tax without representation'.

- He made and then acted on the unpopular decision by throwing the tea overboard. He knew this would be considered an act of treason and he knew the punishment for this.

- He explained the decision to the people and won their support and approval. This was later proven by the fact that many people risked their own lives to warn him of his impending arrest.

Authentic leadership is about making the tough decisions. Once a decision is made, you then have an obligation to communicate it effectively and to win the support and approval of people. If Adams had missed this vital step, who knows how different American history could have been?

This chapter focuses on how you can engage people to follow you—to be inspired, and to be inspiring.

Your storytelling style

Before you start using stories in business it is important to understand your typical storytelling style. Your storytelling style is determined by two factors: how purposeful you are with your stories and how engaging your stories are.

When you tell a story, do you have very high clarity on what message you are trying to get across? Are you clear on what the purpose of your story is, or are you not that sure?

When you deliver your story, how engaging is it? Are people with you all the way or have they stopped listening well before you have stopped talking?

The four styles are shown in the following illustration.

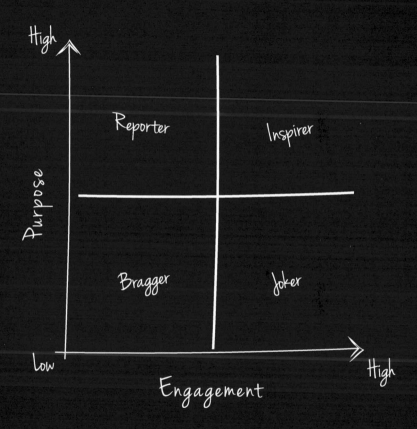

The **Bragger**[1] storyteller tends to tell very longwinded stories about themselves and their successes, with a focus on 'the good old days' or sport. The Bragger's stories are very low on engagement and provide no clarity around their purpose. It seems the only message they are trying to get across is how great they are. Stories are often about yourself, but you need to be careful that they don't take on a 'bragging' feel. You can normally avoid this with a healthy level of self-deprecating behaviour.

The **Joker** tells lots of really funny, engaging stories that have either low or no purpose, except to make people laugh. It's an admirable aim in life but the Joker misses many amazing opportunities when it comes to storytelling in business. The biggest opportunity they miss is connecting their stories to a business message, because people remember the story and its humour, but don't remember the message.

The Joker can also tend to use humour for humour's sake, which again runs the risk of detracting from the message.

The **Reporter** is the most common storyteller style in business. The Reporter's stories tend to have lots of facts and figures and statistics in them. Reporters also tend to use a lot of case studies, thinking they act in the same way as stories, and they tend to use a lot of business examples. This means their stories are less engaging. So while the Reporter may have clarity on their purpose for the story, overall their stories are very low on engagement.

The **Inspirer** is crystal clear on their purpose in using and narrating stories, and because of this their stories are highly engaging. They achieve this high engagement because they are not afraid to share personal stories and they know exactly how they can connect a personal story with a business message.

---

[1] In *Hooked*, a book I co-authored, I used the term 'Avoider' for this style of storyteller but I have since started referring to this as Bragger because I think it is a more accurate description.

You may move around the quadrants but you will most likely have a normal or default style. This may be a case of stating the obvious but the Inspirer is who you should aspire to be.

Your storytelling grapevine

The most efficient and cost-effective communication channel you have at your disposal as a leader is the grapevine. In organisations, the grapevine doesn't need a strategy or action plan, it doesn't need a department to manage it and it can't be controlled. Yet, it can be influenced.

It is worth your while as a leader to ensure that the stories being shared about you on the grapevine (and, whether you realise it or not, stories are being shared about you) are positive. You can do this in two ways: a 'pull' approach or a 'push' approach. Just like in marketing, using a combination of both approaches works best.

THE MOST EFFICIENT AND COST-EFFECTIVE *communication* CHANNEL YOU HAVE AT YOUR DISPOSAL AS A LEADER IS THE GRAPEVINE.

The pull approach involves stories generated by the actions and decisions you make.

The push approach involves stories you choose to proactively share.

Pull stories

You don't have total control of your pull stories because these are the stories people create in their head and share based on your actions and decisions. Stories about you are already out there! People are already sharing stories about you—about your leadership style, about your values, and about what you are like to work for and work with.

When Andrew Thorburn was appointed the new CEO of NAB in 2014, Australia's national newspaper wrote an article on his appointment, and this article was circulated by NAB's internal Yammer network. One employee wrote a comment about how proud she was when she read the article. Andrew responded with a comment of his own, thanking the woman and saying how proud his mum also was of the article.

This was only a small gesture by him but the impact was staggering. Over the next month, I can't tell you how many NAB employees told me that story. All were sharing it because they just thought it was great that a CEO would do that, and they believed that it showed he was a decent, down-to-earth and approachable guy.

Another example of a great pull story comes from Mark Leopold, the corporate affairs director at Readify, an agile and growing technology company. The company's managing director (and part owner) is Graeme Strange. Before Mark joined Readify, he and Graeme had known each other through golf; they'd played at the same club and occasionally bumped into each other.

As MD of Readify, Graeme has always valued people. Readify is built on great technologists; brilliant people who deliver innovative, custom software to help solve business problems. Graeme is not one to rest on success and, instead, is always looking to re-invigorate the company. In his eyes, retaining leadership in a fast-moving industry requires an even faster company.

To sustain growth, Graeme was looking for new ideas and wanted to inject new business thinking into the leadership team. The technology side of the business was strong but the time was right to now increase general business and management skills. Knowing Mark's diverse business background, Graeme asked Mark to consider working at Readify.

Mark was surprised and interested in the idea. However, he had some concerns too. He did not have a background in technology and was also coming from larger 'corporate' type businesses; the idea was attractive but his concern was his own ability to add value in such an environment. Both spent time evaluating options after an initial discussion.

While considering options, Mark reflected on a number of things. A key consideration was Graeme's optimism and confidence in the Readify team.

Mark reflected: 'Looking back, I never remembered Graeme speaking negatively about his team or his company. Never. In truth, neither of us talks much about business on the weekend but when he did, it was positive. This is not always the case—in my experience, some leaders tend to have a more negative outlook.' So Graeme's positive outlook—even when he wasn't 'selling' the merits of Readify—was a big tick.

Mark found the icing on the cake when he attended a company get-together in Queensland prior to formally starting. Graeme had gathered the Readify team for an annual 'kick-off'—a time when the whole company celebrates success and discusses the future. Mark was staggered by the event, and it made him realise he was joining something different—and something a little scary for someone with 20 years' experience in a conservative business environment. The main reason for Mark's reaction was that, numerous times, Graeme divulged very sensitive information about Readify's strategy and pending plans. Mark noted that other organisations would close off such information to a chosen few. But not Graeme, and not Readify.

Graeme asked his employees to keep this information to themselves for a few weeks until it was announced publicly. He didn't ask for trust; he just trusted.

Mark thought this was idiocy and close to madness. He said, 'I am hearing Graeme divulge very sensitive information to over a hundred employees, all with their smart phones in hand—meaning they are only a few taps away from sharing this information across multiple social media sites'.

Mark conveyed that he was amazed that the employees respected Graeme's wish and the information never leaked. Mark shared that story with me to highlight the fact that he joined Readify because it reflected the culture he wanted to be part of. A culture where not only the employees had such high respect for the business but also the MD had such high regard and trust for his employees. This goes some way to explaining Readify's sustainable success.

When Jac Phillips was appointed head of brand and marketing at Bank of Melbourne, she wanted to make it clear to everyone in her new team that she operated by a core set of values—inclusion and respect. One of her first priorities was to sit for an hour with each member of her team to find out what they loved about their job, what they didn't love about their job and what their passions were. She sat beside them, not opposite them, because she wanted to show she meant it when she said she considered this an equal relationship. As a part of these conversations, Jac also included some suppliers who worked closely with the team.

Jac was living her values of respect and inclusivity because her actions were visible—and they were noticed. Her team started to talk about the congruence of her messages and her actions, and told her on many occasions the impact those conversations had. Too many leaders come into an organisation and say all the right things—but then their actions are in total contrast to what they say. These leaders are not being real.

Another example of actions having a greater impact than words comes from the CEO of the Alannah and Madeline Foundation, Judith Slocombe. Judith is a highly successful businesswoman who believes that the success of any organisation relies on every employee's individual contribution. Before the annual staff Christmas party, Judith writes a personal card to every employee and thanks each and every person, individually, for their contribution. This is something she does on her own. Typically the CEO would ask her leadership team or executive assistant for help with this task—perhaps supplying details on what each employee has achieved over the year—but she doesn't need to do that. She understands each individual's contribution deeply.

The organisation has doubled over the past three years and, each Christmas, her support team suggests that Judith may not have the time to write personal cards to every employee. However, each year she does. This is another example of real leadership in action, and again shows how your actions generate stories about your true values, not your espoused values.

It is important to understand that your actions will generate stories. As a leader, be aware of this and work with it. Make sure your actions generate positive stories, not negative stories. Of course, sometimes a negative story is unavoidable, because one action could result in different interpretations. You only have to look at the world of politics to see how one statement or decision can divide a nation. However, you can still do your best to ensure your actions generate stories about the values you want to represent you.

ONE MEMORABLE STORY CAN *transform* YOUR PROFESSIONAL BRAND.

The other way to influence your story grapevine is to actively place stories into it—and this is the push effect.

Push stories

Push stories are those that demonstrate your values and that you strategically share. These stories become a valuable tool for you once you decide to step into real leadership, because one memorable story can transform your professional brand. These stories can be shared in a variety of situations—from one-on-one conversations, to team meetings, to job interviews or in presentations.

Here is an example Basma used in a job interview to demonstrate her leadership style and values:

> Ever since my daughter Millie was born, she has sung. Even though it's a cliché, I can say she was born screaming and hasn't stopped since. From the moment she could talk, she expressed a desire to perform and sing. As early as the lower primary school years, she would tell anyone who would listen that she was going to be a singer when she grew up. I found myself, from her earliest years, strongly pushing her in other directions, telling her how hard it was to make a career in the arts. Yes, I lectured a primary school aged child about career choices. I heard that cliché 'You will need something else to fall back on' come out of my mouth more times than I care to remember. While I paid for singing and piano lessons, I don't think I ever fully appreciated the fire that burned within this young girl to pursue her dreams.

> When it came to choosing a secondary school for Millie, I took her along to a school with a strong reputation in the performing arts, thinking that she would be happiest there, but still secretly wishing that she would find something more 'normal' as a career choice. We sat in the Head of the Middle School's office answering all the standard questions, and he asked, 'What do you want to do when you finish school, Millie?' She looked him straight in the eye and without hesitation said, 'I want to be a singer'. And he looked straight back at her and said, 'Brilliant'.

For me, it was the parenting 'Aha' moment that was long overdue. I was the only person in that office who didn't utterly believe this was her strength and her calling. I changed not only my parenting style at that moment but also my view of the teams I lead. Just as I stopped trying to have the child I wanted and embraced the child I had, I also now pay greater attention to the strengths of the people I lead, and I embrace differences and am mindful of the 'singers' I lead. It has made my style more patient and adaptive, and allowed me to build higher performing teams.

Another example comes from Catherine. Catherine had her sights on bigger and broader roles but the people making the decisions about her career had pigeonholed her in other roles.

One of the characteristics Catherine wanted to get across to her superiors was her ability to take calculated risks, and make tough and quick decisions in high-pressured circumstances. To communicate this she deliberately started sharing the following story in relevant situations:

Ten years ago I found myself scuba diving off the coast of Mexico. It was perfect weather and brilliant conditions. However, five minutes after descending, I got caught in a massive rip. It dragged me for kilometres and split me from my dive group. I was getting banged against rocks and thrown around. At one stage, I vomited into my regulator, which is not an ideal situation when this is your only access to oxygen. As you could imagine, my heart was pumping—which is, again, not ideal because you're using your oxygen supply at a much faster rate.

I emerged from the rip after what seemed like hours—even though it was probably only about ten minutes—and eventually found one of my dive group members underwater. Given the fact that we now had limited air, we surfaced relatively quickly but safely. I remember that feeling of my head eventually breaking the surface of the water and looking around to see the boat…however, there was no boat and no sign of land. We were alone in the vast ocean.

After many years of diving, I'd never encountered this situation before. Out of air, no boat, battered and in searing hot sun and now rough sea ... and no way of communicating.

I had to think fast and quickly get control. I dropped my weight belt and tank to make myself lighter and conserve energy. I filled my buoyancy vest to the max to get my head high above the water and the waves that were crashing down on us, and I tied myself and my dive buddy together.

Two hours later, the boat eventually found us and we were rescued.

I am sharing this with you because I think it captures how I approach leadership challenges in general. I am able to make tough and quick decisions in a crisis, and I have resilience. Even though my experience in Mexico was unbelievably scary at the time, a part of it was absolutely exhilarating. I know in business we will encounter rips and rough seas, and I know I am up for it.

Another example of how to use storytelling to get across your values comes from Tristram Gray, head of human resources at Ericsson for the South-East Asia and Oceania region. Tristram is based in Singapore with a diverse team, and he wanted his team to know the importance of asking the right questions so that you solve customer's real problems. This was something Tristram valued, and he used this story to convey this value to his team:

My family and I moved to Singapore in early 2012 and soon after my wife, Michelle, needed to take our eight-year-old son, Harry, to the doctor as he had developed a fever. The only appointment time she could get was 8 o'clock in the evening.

The doctor assessed Harry and prescribed some antibiotics. Michelle asked the doctor's receptionist where the nearest pharmacy was. The receptionist provided directions to the nearest pharmacy, which turned out to only be a couple of kilometres away.

Michelle and Harry set off and within ten minutes arrived at the pharmacy, only to find that it was closed, and had been so since 6 pm.

Frustrated, they returned to the doctor's surgery and asked the receptionist why she had sent them to a closed pharmacy.

The receptionist replied that Michelle had asked where the nearest pharmacy was, and this was the nearest one. She then gave Michelle directions to the nearest *open* pharmacy, which was a little further away, and Michelle was able to purchase the medicine Harry required.

This made me think about how many times we provide answers or solutions to the problem or issue that is being presented to us, rather than taking the time to ask the right questions to ensure we answer or resolve the real problem.

Every day we have opportunities to send our customers to the nearest closed pharmacy or the nearest open pharmacy. By asking the right questions, imagine the difference we can make.

This is another great example of using a personal story to demonstrate what you believe in and value.

Coming up with push stories

The first place to start when trying to come up with your own push stories is determining what you want to be known for. Think about what is important to you, what your core values are. Write them down on a piece of paper. Don't try to list too many values or you'll end up being known for none of them. Instead, choose your top two or three values.

Once you know what you want to be known for, find stories from your past that demonstrate these values. You can do this through taking some time to reflect on your life and then through answering some specific questions. Then, you can actively start to share the stories that demonstrate your values.

This three-step process, outlined in more detail in the following sections, will help you find your stories.

Step 1: This is your life

Pour yourself a cup of coffee, a cup of tea or a glass of wine—the choice is yours. Then grab a blank piece of paper and a pen and find a place where you can work uninterrupted for about 30 minutes. Next, reflect back through your life—from your earliest memory to today—and start writing your most powerful memories down. Whatever memories come to you. Do not analyse what you are thinking about or if it is relevant—just write it down.

When I did this for the first time, some of my memories were:

- falling out of a tree when I was five and cutting my knee open
- hitting a girl in Grade 2 and having Mum called to the school
- wearing long socks instead of ankle socks on my first day of secondary school
- my fiancé leaving me for another woman six months before our wedding
- running 32 kilometres across King Island
- doing the Oxfam 100-kilometre challenge
- not getting the promotion I thought I was going to get.

Give yourself ten minutes to make your list. After the ten minutes is up, go back to each one and, in a word or two, describe what the memory was about—what it represents overall. So, for example, the descriptions I added to my list of memories were:

- falling out of a tree when I was five and cutting my knee open—ADVENTURE
- hitting a girl in Grade 2 and having Mum called to the school—STANDING UP

- wearing long socks instead of ankle socks on my first day of secondary school — FITTING IN

- my fiancé leaving me for another woman six months before our wedding — RESILIENCE

- running 32 kilometres across King Island — CHALLENGE

- doing the Oxfam 100 kilometre challenge — CHALLENGE

- not getting the promotion I thought I was going to get — RESILIENCE.

The final stage of this process is to identify any themes or words that occur in the descriptions more than once. For me, resilience and challenge each appeared twice. Just circle or highlight any words that appear more than once.

Step 2: Q&A

Now I want you to go a bit deep with your memories. On another piece of paper, write down your answers to the following activities and questions:

- What experience in your early life had the biggest influence or impact on you? Describe what it was, why it had such an impact and how it influences you today.

- Describe a recent experience that has made you proud. What was it and why did it make you proud?

- Describe three times when you felt fulfilled, content or happy. What were you doing? How were you feeling? Why do you value this so much?

- Describe one of your biggest regrets. What is it? Why do you regret it? Has it changed the choices you make today?

- Have you ever been in a situation where you have had a clash of values? What were they and what did you decide to do?

- Have you done anything that scared the hell out of you but you did it anyway? What was it and what process did you go through to overcome your fear?

For example, recently, my youngest daughter, Jess, advised us that she wanted to participate in the Shave for a Cure fundraiser, which raises money for leukaemia and, as you may know, would involve her shaving her head. As her mother, I was both proud and horrified. I must admit I did try to talk her out of it by saying, 'But what will you look like?' She replied by telling me that, unlike Alex (her elder sister, who is the ballet dancer), she didn't care what she looked like. This is slightly harsh on her elder sister, but true. Then she asked me, 'What about the kids who get leukaemia? They don't get a choice in what they look like because they just lose their hair.' My horror subsided into absolute pride. Her words reinforced to me the importance having a purpose and showing leadership around that, regardless of the consequences.

Step 3: Aligning your stories with what you want to be known for

Go back to the piece of paper where you wrote down the values you want to be known for, and then go back over what you wrote down for Steps 1 and 2 to see if any of the examples you have described demonstrate these values.

If they do, you have a suite of stories you can actively start putting onto your personal grapevine. I encourage you to share them at every relevant opportunity. In presentations, job interviews, team meetings and coaching sessions, and with clients, peers, your team and your leaders. Just ensure you are sharing these stories in a way that is authentic and relevant.

If you are looking at your list of values you want to be known for and none of the examples and stories you listed in Steps 1 and 2 match, you need to ask yourself a very tough question. Are the values you listed actually the values you espouse and your values in action?

The organisational grapevine

In my practice, I work a lot with senior executives in charge of culture, in charge of leadership, in charge of employee engagement, in charge of communications, and in charge of strategy. All these are critical areas of focus within organisations. However, I think organisations are overlooking perhaps the most critical platform that has an impact across the entire organisation: the organisational grapevine.

The organisational grapevine is in every single organisation; every single employee is part of it, every single employee actively engages in it, and every single employee is affected by it. Yet very few organisations give it the attention it deserves. This needs to change. While the grapevine was always powerful, technology and all forms of social media have been giving it significantly more power.

If the grapevine were a piece of hardware, the software would be stories. If the grapevine is left unattended, the vast majority of stories in the grapevine will be negative, and while you can't control the grapevine, you can certainly influence the stories that are fuelling it.

The organisation that understands the power of the grapevine and takes active and strategic steps to influence it can experience huge advantages in employee engagement, strategy awareness and organisational or cultural change.

In this context, it's worth looking at the evolution of organisational change. In the 1980s and '90s, cultural change followed a similar format—one known as the 'rollout'. Corporate values and mission statements were emblazoned on beautifully designed wall posters. Along with the wall posters, employees would usually receive a mouse pad or a coffee mug with the organisational values printed on them. Business cards often had the mission or vision statement printed on the reverse side. They were literally rolled out through the organisation via a communication cascade starting from the CEO and moving down.

The intention here was good, and some companies did experience success with this format. Values and mission statements that were visible at every employee's work desk did result in many employees being able to recite the corporate values and mission statement. Unfortunately, very few knew what they actually meant.

The next wave in the corporate cultural revolution saw the move from 'rollouts' to 'road shows', or a blend of the two. People started to realise that the cascade communication approach did not seem to be working, for several reasons. Many of the messages were being lost in translation and many leaders lacked the communication skills needed to connect with their staff.

The solution was to get only the executive leadership team out talking to the employees. Due to the vast number of employees, this was often done via a variety of 'town hall' meetings, where members of the executive team would fly into locations around the country delivering the messages of organisational change to up to a few hundred people at a time. The meetings normally consisted of communicating the reason for the change, what was going to change, the process for change, how the change was going to be measured and how everyone would love their jobs more.

This approach, again, was based on good intentions but had limited success. Often nothing would change after the execs flew in with their 'Are you on the bus or not?' type talk, and then flew out again. Ultimately, nothing much changed because this one-off communication may motivate for a day or a week, but what happens after that? Employees need to be motivated and engaged day-in and day-out, and developing this engagement is not just the job of the senior executive team but also of all leaders.

THE ORGANISATION THAT UNDERSTANDS THE *power* OF THE GRAPEVINE AND TAKES ACTIVE AND STRATEGIC STEPS TO *influence* IT CAN EXPERIENCE HUGE ADVANTAGES IN EMPLOYEE ENGAGEMENT, STRATEGY AWARENESS AND ORGANISATIONAL OR CULTURAL CHANGE.

Some of the shifts I have discussed—such as the unique challenges generation Y brings to the workforce, the concept of the three brains and the exponential growth of technology—will significantly affect the future of organisational change. The evolution organisational change will continue to go through is not dissimilar to the evolution of hardware and software. Each new version should bring a better way of operating by offering enhancements and fixing bugs of the past.

This need to improve on the way we undertake organisational change is brought about predominately by the generational and technological shifts occurring. With generation Y becoming the most dominant generation, organisations need to address the accompanying challenges — including the greater expectations they have of their employers and the focus of loyalty shifting to purpose and lifestyle.

The exponential growth in technology has resulted in far easier access to information, and made it significantly harder for leaders to have an impact.

Organisations need to dramatically alter the way they lead and communicate. They need to obsess about engaging the whole brain and to communicate in a collective way, not in the traditional cascade or collaborative approach. For organisations to be successful in their organisational change, they need to move from the 'rollout' or 'road show' mindset to the 'real thing' mindset, upgrade to the new version and start using storytelling strategically.

ORGANISATIONS NEED TO *dramatically* ALTER THE WAY THEY LEAD AND COMMUNICATE. THEY NEED TO OBSESS ABOUT ENGAGING THE WHOLE BRAIN AND TO *communicate* IN A COLLECTIVE WAY, NOT IN THE TRADITIONAL CASCADE OR COLLABORATIVE APPROACH.

The following illustration compares these three versions, and the approaches and expectations of each.

Version	1.0 – Rollouts	2.0 – Roadshows	3.0 – Real Thing
Platform	Coffee mugs + mouse pads	Power Point + Town Hall meetings	Stories + the Grapevine
Communication approach	Cascade – one way	Collaborative – two way	Collectic – multiple ways
Engaged the	Head	Head + Heart	Head, Heart + Gut
Dominant generation	Baby Boomers	Gen X	Gen Y
Loyalty focus	Company	Company + Lifestyle	Purpose + Lifestyle
Expectation of employees	Low	Medium	High
Access to information	Limited	Easy	Inundated
Ability to impact	Easy	Medium	Hard

Strategic storytelling

Strategic, authentic, storytelling can be employed once you have clarity on the strategic direction or cultural change that needs to happen. The strategy involves four stages:

1 equipping your leaders and influencers with the skill

2 capturing stories

3 sharing stories

4 generating stories.

Authenticity is at the heart of this entire strategy, as shown in the illustration on page 101.

Skill

Formalising the business storytelling process and providing leaders with the necessary training is important—this allows them to skilfully apply the process.

Avoid training leaders purely according to hierarchy. Instead, identify and include key influencers in the organisation who could also be trained in storytelling to help achieve the change. And also include support people in the training, such as internal communications and human resources specialists, so they can support and encourage the use of storytelling.

Give leaders the opportunity to practise their stories and to obtain feedback.

Capture

You will need to develop formal and informal strategies to capture stories. The focus of the stories you capture should celebrate the past, acknowledge the present and paint the future. Therefore, it is critical to capture stories from a diverse range of people, including people of different age, tenure, position, location and race.

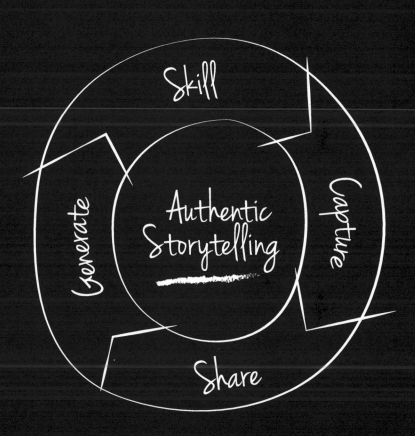

You will also need to provide leaders with the tools, techniques and time to effectively listen to stories, because to be a good storyteller you need to be a great story listener.

Share

To encourage the sharing of stories throughout your organisation, you will need to create a culture that supports the use of organisational storytelling. This is best achieved via role modelling, starting with the CEO and senior leadership team, and through sharing stories in all formal and informal communications.

Find multiple channels to relay stories to other leaders, employees and customers. Your aim with sharing stories is to influence the grapevine without controlling it. Stories should encourage the behaviours and culture you want.

Generate

Understand the concept of 'pull' stories and how the actions and decisions of your leaders and employees generate stories. Empower all employees to deliver on the promise of the new strategy or culture, which will generate positive stories. Use stories to generate further stories and be aware of the ripple effect of stories—and know how to maximise that impact.

The stages of capture, share and generate are not linear and should be conducted in parallel and in an ongoing, circular fashion.

Top 10 storytelling mistakes

When adopting such a storytelling strategy, leaders and organisations often make some avoidable, yet common, mistakes. Here are the top 10:

1 Not having clarity on what type of culture the organisation wants to cultivate.

2 Expecting leaders to use storytelling in business skilfully and effectively but not investing in their training so they can learn the skill.

3 Only training leaders based on position and ignoring other key influencers.

4 Calling something a story without it being a story at all.

5 Developing stories by committee.

6 Attempting to come up with one story to communicate everything to everyone.

7 Capturing stories by going out to employees and asking them to 'Share your story here...'

8 Over-engineering each element and not trusting the process.

9 Not being authentic and transparent with stories and communications.

10 Not acknowledging the current reality and trying to sugar-coat negatives.

Top tips for storytelling

The following specific storytelling tips are aimed at helping your stories be more real and helping you share your stories in a more engaging and authentic way.

Tip 1: Make it personal

The real power in using stories in business is to use a personal story and attach it to a business message.

Cindy Batchelor is Executive General Manager, NAB Business. She is a long-term client of mine and a woman I admire and respect. Cindy is tall, and extremely fit and healthy. She plays basketball, runs half-marathons and recently completed the Kokoda Trail. She is also strong and forthright in her opinion and is not afraid of showing emotion. Cindy understands the power of storytelling and, if you ever have the pleasure of hearing Cindy present, you will no doubt hear her tell a story—and a personal story at that.

Here is an example of a story Cindy shares often to deliver the message of how important it is to be positive and to 'reframe' any situation:

> Two years ago I lost my husband in a tragic paragliding accident. In our time of dealing with this loss, my youngest son Billy said to me that his greatest fear was, 'If it could happen to Dad, it could happen to you'. As a parent, this is a tough one to respond to—there are no guarantees in life.
>
> Ten months after John's accident I was involved in a car accident while driving home from work. I had stopped at the shop on the way home to pick up some groceries and rang my eldest son Jackson when I was about five minutes away to get him to meet me outside to help with the groceries. Two minutes from home I was 'T-boned' in my car and instantaneously six airbags deployed. In a sliding doors moment I pulled up just before I ran into a power pole. The car was a total write-off but luckily both the other driver and I walked away a little bruised but okay.
>
> The only thing that was going through my mind at the time was the memory of Billy saying, 'If it could happen to Dad, it could happen to you' and thinking that at that moment Jackson was standing outside at home waiting for me—and I was not going be turning up anytime soon.
>
> A lady walking by allowed me to use her mobile phone to ring Jackson. He was 500 metres away and he immediately ran across the park in his school uniform and socks to find me. As you can imagine, I was pretty upset and I just said how scared I was of what could have happened. Jackson gave me a hug and calmly said to me, 'Mum, you can't think of it like that. You need to think of it like this—you drive a safe car and the airbags worked.' I just hugged him with pride about his perfect, powerful and positive response.

I am sharing this with you because every day when I am faced with the challenges of running this business, I often ask myself, 'How would Jackson reframe this?'

I spoke to Cindy about how and why she used such a personal story. She said,

It was a few weeks after this incident when I needed to address my team about the challenges of delivering outcomes in the face of obstacles and Jackson's words of wisdom came back to me. So I told this story and introduced the notion of 'reframing' as a concept in business. Due to the power of storytelling to get your message across, 'reframing' quickly became the language of positivity in my business. This story has had the most incredible impact on my business and the way I connect with my people. There is a real strength in showing vulnerability as a leader.

Another example of sharing a personal story to great effect comes from Jenni Coles, director of care homes and rehabilitation at Bupa Care Services in Auckland, New Zealand.

Jenni used this story to communicate 'extraordinary'—one of Bupa's organisational values. Bupa wanted to communicate to their people that extraordinary meant going above and beyond. This is how Jenny did so:

My dad had six young children when he was diagnosed with a severe heart infection. This resulted in him being one of the first people in NZ to have both a human-to-human heart valve replacement and a pacemaker.

He could have become a cardiac cripple and given up work. But he didn't. He continued to work and support our family for the next 20 years.

Dad was a county engineer and responsible for roads and bridges for a large rural area. Within that area, there were about 100 small old one-lane wooden bridges. These needed to be replaced because they were dangerous for the stock trucks and families, but the county didn't have sufficient funding to replace them all.

So Dad researched the options, including visiting Australia to see the latest methods, and decided the best approach was to replace the bridges with concrete two-lane bridges. What he did next was extraordinary. He went above and beyond. In our own backyard he built a concrete plant, powered by an engine from a steam train, and got to work creating all the bridge piles and bridge spans for the 100 bridges.

When I think about my dad, a lasting image I have is of him standing beside a truck loaded with the makings of a bridge with a huge smile on this face.

I see my Dad as extraordinary... he battled through severe illness to provide for our family and he followed his desire to ensure our community had safe roads and bridges. Those bridges are still there today and will be for the next 100 years.

We might not be building physical bridges at Bupa but every day we have the opportunity to be extraordinary. To go above and beyond, to be the best we can dream to be—like my Dad did—and to deliver outstanding results both big and small.

You will notice with all these stories that, although they have a personal connection, people are not sharing their most intimate secrets. It is this misconception that often frightens people away from using storytelling in business—but business storytelling is not about that. Everyday stories are actually the most powerful, because these are the stories that people connect to.

Sharing personal stories that show vulnerability can be very powerful, especially for leaders in organisations. Sharing stories that are embarrassing, challenging, sad or hurtful, and then sharing the wisdom you gained from these events in your life, can be incredibly inspiring for your team. But, you need to have reconciled with the event that happened before you share it with others.

If you are still angry or bitter about what happened, this emotion will come out and it won't be inspiring. If time has not allowed you to heal from the events and the emotion is too raw for you, this will come out when you start to share your story. Some emotion in telling a story is brilliant; emotion that is too raw will result in both you and your audience becoming very uncomfortable. If this happens, you may not achieve the result you wanted when telling the story. You may have wanted to inspire people, but instead all you may receive is sympathy.

Many senior leaders today are being encouraged to share their 'leadership story'. This story is typically a major event in their life that has had such an impact that it has influenced the person they are today and the way they lead.

I was once called into an organisation by their events manager, who wanted the executive manager to share his leadership story and wanted me to help him with this. In our time together, he told me his story—the one that they wanted him to share in front of more than 200 leaders. The raw emotion was visible and I could tell he was uncomfortable sharing it. He still had not recovered from the events that took place. Sharing that story would have been a mistake. So I worked with him on another story that he was more comfortable sharing but that would still produce the same outcome.

As the storyteller, you have the ultimate final decision on what stories you share and who you share them with. Personal stories of hurt and vulnerability are very powerful. But only when you have reconciled with the past events will you be able to share your insights and learnings. When that happens, your stories will become very inspiring.

So first repair and then share your story.

Tip 2: Use humour wisely

In an effort to be more engaging, many people try to make their stories funny. Nothing is wrong with sharing a funny story—that people love humorous stories is undeniable. So humour definitely has its place in business storytelling and in business presentations and I encourage you to use it purposefully and appropriately.

But how can you use humour effectively in your stories? And what should you avoid?

Do use humour to break the ice

Humour has been scientifically proven to have physical benefits. The old adage that 'laughter is the best medicine' has wisdom. Laughter has been proven to:

- relax the whole body
- decrease stress hormones
- trigger the release of endorphins, the body's natural feel-good hormones.

So getting your audience to laugh sooner rather than later, and you also being able to laugh along, is related to these three physical benefits. It will relax you, which is great for helping to ensure you narrate your story in your natural style. It will decrease your stress, which is important if you are feeling a bit anxious about your story. And it will trigger those endorphins in your audience and get them feeling good towards you.

I did some work with a group of four young graduates who had to present at their company's yearly conference. The four graduates came together beforehand to practise their

TOP TIPS FOR STORYTELLING:
- Make it personal
- Use humour wisely
- Use emotion over data
- Start smart
- End smarter

stories. One of the grads, Scott, was really nervous, even at this practice session. About halfway through the story he'd included a humorous line — at which we all laughed. After that point, Scott continued on with his story but in a more natural tone. When everyone laughed and Scott himself also laughed, it relaxed him and his story just seemed to flow better after that.

What we then did with Scott's story was to use that funny line much earlier in the story. This helped Scott, who was still very nervous, relax into his story significantly earlier, making for a much more engaging story.

Do use humour to bring in humility

When you are sharing stories about yourself, you probably want to avoid telling stories about how great you are. Even if the story does involve you doing great things, you can use humour to bring in humility. This does not mean you have to belittle your achievements but some self-deprecating humour never goes astray.

Don't use humour for the sake of it

Humour for the sake of it is self-indulgent and will distract from the purpose. If you use humour without a purpose, you slip into the Joker style of storytelling and your message may be lost.

Don't use humour that can be interpreted as sexist or racist

The key word in this tip is 'interpreted'. You may have seen many people overstep this mark without realising it. One client told a story about going to buy a computer for his wife and then proceeded to go on about how technically illiterate she was and how he had to do everything when it came to technology. So, in itself, the story may not have been overly sexist but it would be fair to say that he lost 50 per cent of his audience (the women), right there.

Political humour is also risky because it has the potential to divide your audience.

Tip 3: Use emotion over data

Another common mistake leaders make with storytelling is they include too many numbers in their story. I have a theory that you should try to avoid using numbers, unless absolutely necessary. You may need some numbers to set context such as 'five years ago' or 'when I was ten', but too many numbers can distract from your story. When you use numbers in your story, your audience naturally assumes they are important so unconsciously they try to remember all the numbers. This distracts from their emotional engagement in your story.

As I discussed previously, in business most leaders have a reporter style and by default use a lot of numbers or stats in their stories. However, stories are effective because, if done right, they tap into our emotion. The more facts, figures, stats and so on you have in your stories, the less room you have left for emotion.

Tip 4: Start smart

'Four years ago I went on a trip to Vietnam with my family in August. Actually I think it was five years ago. Anyway before we went on the trip. Oh, sorry, it was four years ago and it wasn't August it was September. Well, I think we left late August but came back in September — actually it was all of September because I know we were over there when the grand final was on and that is the last weekend in September...' Have I lost you already? I bet I have.

You would be amazed at how many people start their stories like this and, believe me, people have stopped listening before they even get through a few sentences. I call this the 'Grandpa Simpson start'. If you are a fan of *The Simpsons* you will know that Grandpa's stories often start with banal information—for example, 'I had an onion on my belt, which was the style at the time. They didn't have white onions because of the war. The only thing you could get was those big yellow ones...'

Your start should be short and sharp. The best formula is to quickly establish the time and place, such as 'When I was a kid I grew up on a farm...' or 'Three years ago I ran a half marathon...'

The quality of their beginnings in one of the reasons we are seduced by the 'off the cuff' stories good leaders use—that is, how they start their stories. The start of your story should be very conversational such as, 'That reminds me of a time when...' or 'As a kid I grew up in the country and...' These conversational starts do two things. They are efficient, so they save time but, most importantly, they hook people in immediately. Imagine being in a business meeting and someone starts talking with, 'This reminds me of a time when I went scuba diving'. As humans, we are hardwired to listen to stories so we intrinsically engage when someone starts to tell a story, and starts well.

Tip 5: End smarter

The way you end a story will make or break it. Your stories should link to your purpose in a subtle way. You can't afford to be too direct—for example, by ending the story with comments like, 'So the moral of the story is...' or 'So what this means is that I need you to start doing x, y and z'. Use more inviting hooks such as 'Imagine what we could achieve if...' or 'I invite you to consider...'

You also need to slow down at the end of your story, and you can take guidance from the music world here and remember the term *ritardando*. *Ritardando* is an Italian word that means gradually getting slower; it is usually abbreviated to 'rit'. A rit can be in the middle of a musical piece or at the end.

Similarly, in your storytelling you can have a rit in the middle of your story, when you slow down to make a point, and a rit at the end of your stories, again to make a point and signal that it is the end of the story. A rit can take the form of appropriate pauses and literally speaking slower. Without being too prescriptive, you could have a brief one-second pause before your final sentence, say your final sentence slowly and then have a longer pause at the end. So I think one of the ways to make your story a hit is to end with a rit.[2]

When it comes to storytelling, I believe the ending of your story is critical—and this point in the story does involve a lot of hidden traps. Let's look at the two most common rookie mistakes and the best ways to avoid them.

Rookie mistake number 1—not stopping

Knowing when to stop is critical. Every story has a bell curve of emotion. By stopping right on the top of the curve, you get maximum impact. If you continue beyond this point, you actually get diminishing returns. The audience gets bored, misses the point or wonders when you are going to finish. Most people keep going longer than they should because they think their audience isn't getting it. They got it but now you are losing them. If you have teenage children, you will no doubt have experienced this dropping off in interest—when you believe you're still imparting words of wisdom and they walk off saying, 'Yeah, I get it. You don't have to go on about it.' Your audience is thinking the same thing—they're just more polite to your face than your children.

Many people share their story and then it just seems to merge into the next thing they are saying. The story doesn't seem to have a distinct end. When this happens your audience is just left wondering, 'What was that about?'

---

[2]Sorry—that's the best rhyming I could do.

To avoid this, know what your last sentence is and make sure you stop after it, pause and then segue into what you are saying next. And as Dorothy Sarnoff, an American operatic soprano, said, 'Make sure you have finished speaking before your audience has finished listening'.

Rookie mistake number 2—being too directive

Being too directive—for example, telling your audience what you want them to take away from the story—does not work.

In traditional storytelling, the stories often end with a 'the moral of the story is...' type sentence. This is a directive ending—you're telling the audience what to think or what to take away from the story—yet this doesn't work in business. In business, you have to trust that your audience understands your message. This is hard for most leaders to do, because we have been taught to spell everything out for our audience instead of trusting and respecting their intelligence.

If you are going to be directive at the end because you think your audience won't get it, don't even bother using a story—just tell them what you want. But remember, stories do a lot of heavy lifting for you and the white space at the end of a story is when your audience is relating the story back to them—in effect, creating their own stories. If you immediately jump into directive mode, you have gone back to command and control as opposed to engage and enrol.

Chapter 5

Presenting the real you on stage

Like it or not, every time you present, you are being judged. Your audience will be critiquing not only your presentation style but also your ability as a leader. So if presenting is part of what you do, your presentation can affect, either negatively or positively, your future success and how people see you as a leader.

If you have senior leadership ambitions, it's imperative that you become an inspiring presenter. Organisations want inspiring leaders. Why? Because inspiring leaders engage and motivate a workforce, increase productivity, and attract and retain talented people.

Just look at Barack Obama. He won the US presidential election in 2008 because people believed he would be an inspiring leader, largely because he was an inspiring presenter.

Every time you present, you have an opportunity to increase your leadership presence. So it is worth investing time preparing for your presentation, and determining what will give you the biggest impact or the greatest return on your investment.

Due to the critical importance of presenting I have dedicated a fair number of pages in this book to it. Although the chapter title references the stage, keep in mind that you do not have to physically be on a stage for parts to be relevant. Your stage could be the boardroom or your stage could be around the table at your next team meeting. Your stage could be literal or lateral, and the information in this chapter is relevant regardless of whether you are speaking to thousands or to your team.

So where to begin? First, resist the urge to open up PowerPoint or Keynote and start tapping away. Whenever I have to do a presentation, I go to my favourite cafe and map out my presentation on a single piece of paper.

Over the years I've developed a winning formula for my presentations. I used to always start with the key messages I wanted to convey, but I have since realised there is an earlier place to start—purpose.

This chapter is aimed at providing you with techniques and a framework to help you prepare for your presentation and have the best possible shot of presenting the real you on stage.

EVERY TIME YOU PRESENT, YOU HAVE AN OPPORTUNITY TO INCREASE YOUR *leadership* PRESENCE. SO IT IS WORTH INVESTING TIME PREPARING FOR YOUR PRESENTATION, AND DETERMINING WHAT WILL GIVE YOU THE BIGGEST IMPACT OR THE GREATEST RETURN ON YOUR INVESTMENT.

Start with the why

In chapter 4, I cover Simon Sinek's ideas about understanding the importance of 'why' you do something. In his simple, yet powerful and inspirational TED talk, 'Start With Why', Simon Sinek starts by drawing a circle around the question 'Why?' He then states his main point, 'People don't buy what you do; they buy why you do it'. The 'why' should be at the centre of everything you do. If you have not seen this TED talk, I recommend you watch it at some stage.[1]

The question of 'why?' is exactly where you have to start if you want to determine the purpose of your presentation.

Understand the purpose for your audience

Spending a few minutes on understanding why you are presenting is definitely worthwhile. Doing so will help you gain clarity and will form the foundation of how you build your presentation.

To identify the purpose of your presentation, ask yourself the following four questions:

What do I want my audience to *think*?

What do I want my audience to *feel*?

What do I want my audience to *do*?

What *problem* am I solving for my audience?

Obviously the purpose of your presentation will change every time you do a different presentation, even if it is similar content. So you'll need to ask yourself these questions for each and every presentation you do.

Ask yourself this: at the end of your presentation, what do you want your audience to do? What is it you want to achieve? Before you start thinking about your content

---

[1]To find this talk, search online for 'Simon Sinek why'.

and arranging it into PowerPoint slides, you have to think about 'why' you are presenting. What's the purpose of your presentation?

Understand the purpose for you

I worked with a client who was acting in the role of senior executive. She was going through the formal process of applying for the role she was acting in and her company was also interviewing several external candidates. While she was in the final stages of the interviewing process, she had to do a presentation to the board. I worked with her on her presentation, starting with the why. The purpose for the board was that they needed a high-level overview of the strategy and they wanted to feel confident that this was the right approach. My client also identified a purpose for her—and perhaps a hidden purpose for the board. Like it or not, coincidentally or not, this was a pseudo test and would informally became part of the decision process to identify if she was suitable to hold the senior executive role permanently.

Understanding this influenced the way we structured the presentation. She knew there was a chance that questions from certain board members could drag her into providing technical solutions, whereas she wanted to remain strategic. So we crafted appropriate responses if those situations occurred.

She knew she would be presenting to the board after hours of previous presentations, so she ditched the PowerPoint and went with an approach that would be refreshing and would introduce a change of pace.

She spent more time than usual identifying questions she thought the board would ask and worked on thorough and elegant responses for each of those.

While talking about purpose, one other aspect is worth a mention—the 'listening cost' of the room. If you are a

CEO or a senior leader and you are presenting to 50 or 200 or more of your leaders, think about how much you are actually paying these people to sit and listen to you. Even if the number is lower, considering the 'listening cost' is important. On average, your leaders may earn about $100 an hour. If you have 100 such leaders in the room listening to you for an hour, that is a $10000 'listening cost'. When you think about this, you would want to be good.

I hear many leaders comment on external speakers who are charging that amount, saying something along the line of, 'They better be good for that money'—and they have a point. If you're paying an external speaker $10000 to do a 60-minute keynote, you expect them to be good. You could rightly expect them to be brilliant. But shouldn't we also place that same expectation on ourselves when we consider the 'listening cost' of the people sitting in the room? Not to mention what collectively the people listening could all achieve with those 100 hours. If we consider this aspect for meetings as well as presentations, we may start having shorter meetings and only invite the people who absolutely need to be there.

So now that I have added all that extra pressure, let's make your presentations rock and worth the 'listening cost'.

Once you understand your purpose, you must spend some time looking at this purpose from your audience's perspective. You would be surprised how many presenters don't do this, or only do so at a surface level. But to be a more engaging presenter, you need to go beyond the surface level with an audience analysis and go to a deeper level.

First, the surface level. At this level you do need to understand a few things:

- Who are they?
- How many people are attending?

- What time of day will you be presenting? (After lunch or late afternoon?)

- Will you have to overcome any possible distractions? (For example, lunch being served.)

Then go beyond this and get to a deeper level. Following are some questions worth considering. You may not be able to answer them all and some may be irrelevant. If you don't know your audience at all, speak to someone who does know them and can give you insights into the questions.

Some questions worth thinking about include:

- What problems are you solving (if any)?

- What type of relationship (if any) do you have with your audience?

- What motivates them?

- What do they want from your presentation?

- What are three current challenges or concerns relevant to them?

- Do they want to be there?

- Do they really want to be there or are they expected to be there?

- How will they receive your messages?

- Is there a chance some will see your presentation in a negative light?

- What do you want them to think differently about after your presentation?

- What do you want them to 'do' differently, if anything?

- What do you want them to 'feel' differently?

When I run presentation workshops and take leaders through this exercise, without fail they gain an insight they had not thought of. So I encourage you to ask yourself these questions every time you present.

Your messages

Once you have clarity on your purpose and you have performed your audience analysis, you then need to think about your messages. Think of a target, with the content of your presentation representing the different rings in the target. The outer ring contains all the messages that your audience could know, the middle ring contains all the messages your audience should know, and in the centre are the messages your audience must know. Although you can easily fall into the trap of thinking all your messages are important, trying to communicate ten messages will most likely end with your audience remembering maybe only one or two (or none).

The pigs in George Orwell's *Animal Farm* eventually came up with the single commandment, 'All animals are equal, but some animals are more equal than others'. But I'm not even going to pretend all messages are created equal. Some are just more important than others.

A good practice to get into is to write down all your messages and then prioritise them into the 'must knows', 'should knows' and 'could knows' (as shown in the following table). Then time will dictate how much you cover on each. But you also have other ways to get all the messages across. Perhaps the 'should knows' could be covered off in a question and answer session and the 'could knows' could be sent in a follow-up email after the presentation.

121

Distinguishing between 'must knows', 'should knows' and 'could knows'

Message	Must know	Should know	Could know
1			
2			
3			
4			
5			
6			
7			
8			
9			
10			

'Bumper sticker' your message

Once you have written your messages down and prioritised them, think about how you can 'bumper sticker' your message. Here is a chance for you to move away from the corporate jargon, which has a tendency to bounce off people's heads, and trade that jargon for something that gets into their head, their heart or their gut. This is a chance to have a bit of fun, take a little risk and make your messages 'sticky'.

Look at your messages and ask yourself, 'If they were bumper stickers, what would they be?'

For example, Brian was a senior manager who was trying to communicate to his team that, no matter the communication material they were producing, most people were accessing this material on their smart phones. This meant his team needed to consider this during the design stage. He had written down his message as 'Think of size when designing'. However, he bumper stickered his message to 'size matters'. A little bit risqué perhaps, but a bit of fun and, most importantly, memorable.

When I work with sales teams on how to use storytelling in sales, my main message is, 'When you are selling, reduce the focus on all the facts about the product and sell the value through storytelling, which will increase your sales'. When I bumper sticker that message, it translates to: 'Facts tell; stories sell'.

By bumper stickering your message, you are creating two versions of how you can communicate the message — the business version and the bumper sticker version. The idea is to use both, or to keep both in mind and use each one depending on your audience. However, don't assume that just because you are talking to the board of directors or a senior leadership team they will not appreciate the bumper sticker message. People will most likely remember the bumper sticker and know what it stands for through your business version of the explanation.

Choose your delivery style

One way to help you be more real on stage is to use a variety of pedagogies, or modes of delivery. This not only makes it more interesting for your audience but also allows you to find a pedagogy or two that you feel most comfortable with. Using a pedagogy that you are more comfortable with, and more natural with, will allow you to be more relaxed when presenting and to present the real you on stage.

The next section explores a variety of pedagogies you could start to use.

Stories

So if you have just read the previous chapter, you're probably unsurprised that using stories is at the top of my list of the pedagogies you should use when presenting.

PRESENTING THE REAL YOU ON STAGE:
- Start with the why
- Prioritise your message
- Choose your delivery style
- Avoid PowerPointlessness

In these situations, I believe you should always try to use personal stories to emphasise your messages. I also highly recommend starting your presentation with a story that shows your credibility and passion for what you are about to talk about. Walk on stage and simply start with your story.

For some reason, starting this way seems to freak people out a bit and they are really reluctant to do it. Perhaps because it is so unusual. I often see leaders start a conference by telling people where the toilets are and what to do in case of an emergency. Yes, this information is important and perhaps providing some of it is a legal requirement. But what is more important for you at that moment? Building credibility and instant connection with your audience or making sure they know where the toilets are? You're likely dealing with intelligent adults here and I reckon they may have already figured out where the toilets are. And if they haven't they can probably ask 100 other people before they need to be relying on the person on the stage.

START YOUR PRESENTATION WITH A STORY THAT SHOWS YOUR *credibility* AND *passion* FOR WHAT YOU ARE ABOUT TO TALK ABOUT. WALK ON STAGE AND SIMPLY START WITH YOUR STORY.

So all the 'housekeeping' type information may be important, but it does not have to be the first thing you say. Maybe tell your story first to get connection and engagement and then cover off on the housekeeping.

As discussed in chapter 4, remember that stories don't have to be overly personal, because you may not be comfortable sharing these on stage. But only you can decide what you're comfortable with. If you've reconciled yourself with the events you want to share and feel the story will help your audience engage with your main message, go ahead.

Props

Using props in presentations can be a creative and memorable way to demonstrate a point. For example, Sasha was a project leader who had to present to his senior leadership team the outcomes and recommendations of a project that he and his team had been working on. He was hoping to get funding and resources to implement a new internal employee contacts database and he wanted to emphasise how outdated the current system was.

During the presentation, Sasha held up the *White Pages* telephone directory (which, as you may know, is the size of about two bricks) and asked his audience if they could remember the last time they used one to find the contact details for someone. The answer (as he knew it would be) was years and years ago. He then pulled out his smart phone and said, 'Of course, we all now use one of these'. He went on by saying, 'In our personal life we use a device like this, yet at work we ask our employees to use a device like this'. With that, he dropped the very heavy *White Pages* directory on the table. It landed with a loud thud.

You can see from Sasha's example that the props don't have to be anything grand or outrageous. They just need to provide an opportunity to get your audience's attention, to have an impact and be memorable.

Using a personal prop can also be memorable and provide a great opportunity to bring the whole of you to your presentation — maybe a 'most improved' trophy from your under-11 tennis playing days or a framed photo of your grandparents. You just need to make sure they provide a good link to your main message.

Props can work especially well when combined with a story. Personal props and personal stories are very powerful.

Something unusual

Simply doing something unusual is another underused way to deliver memorable presentations.

About ten years ago I attended a full-day conference with a client. The conference was run by a global logistics company and they had brought about twenty people from around the Australasian region together in the beautiful setting of Indonesia. During the day, each country head would present what they had achieved for the year and cover their targets for next year.

Franc was the leader of the whole team and he was the final speaker. He had to present the overall business results for the last year and the targets for the following year. He had told me before the conference that the targets for the next financial year were a big stretch and he was expecting scepticism from his team, and perhaps even some serious backlash. Being a global company, these targets had been imposed on him and his initial reaction was also of scepticism. He, however, had known about the targets for a couple of weeks so had had time to work though his initial scepticism and was now feeling that the targets were achievable. He was hoping he could fast-track this process for his team so they could spend less time focusing on how the targets could not be achieved — and more time focusing on how they could be achieved.

Franc was co-presenting with one of his team members and what he did I still remember to this day. In fact, it is the only thing I remember from that entire day.

Franc and his co-presenter first went through what had been achieved for the previous twelve months, and then Franc put up the slide showing the following year's targets. Franc let people absorb these targets for about ten seconds and then he just said, 'Those targets are ridiculous. There is no way we can achieve those.' He then walked out the room, closing the door behind him. Everyone in the room just looked at each other wondering what was going on. Franc had a reputation for being a bit of joker but no-one was really sure if he was being serious or not. After about thirty seconds he re-entered the room, talking to himself in a voice that was still audible to the audience. He said, 'Maybe the targets aren't so ridiculous after all. Maybe we could actually achieve them. It will be tough and we will have to do things a bit differently but what if we could achieve them? I think maybe I should give this a go.'

Now, at this stage it was obvious to everyone that this was part of the presentation, but it had the desired effect of fast-tracking the mindset of his team from 'We can't do this' to 'We may able to achieve it'. Total acceptance wasn't that fast and there was certainly discussion about how much of a stretch the stretch targets were, but overall the approach worked. Franc took a risk, did something unusual and memorable, and it worked. More importantly, Franc was a bit of a fun guy. He liked to push the boundaries and not take things too seriously so this was absolutely true to him. The whole time it was the real Franc on stage.

I worked with another senior executive leader who was tasked with introducing the session after lunch. I had worked with him on a personal story he was going to share with his team, and on what he thought was important for leadership to him, to his business and the leaders he led. The setting was a large conference room of approximately 250 people, all sitting at tables of ten.

IF YOU ARE PREPARED TO TAKE A CALCULATED RISK AND DO SOMETHING JUST A LITTLE BIT *unexpected*, YOU CAN HAVE A HUGE IMPACT.

Instead of immediately taking to the stage, he decided to start at the very back of the room. He was wearing a lapel microphone so he was audible but, at the start, no-one knew where he was standing. Everyone was looking around to see where he was, and it only took a few seconds for them to find him at the back of the room. He spoke for about five minutes and slowly made his way to the stage in a bit of a crisscross fashion, walking past most tables as he did so. Doing something just a little bit different combined with a personal story had a big impact.

If you are prepared to take a calculated risk and do something just a little bit unexpected, you can have a huge impact. Take some advice from the 'King', Elvis Presley. He simply said, 'Do something worth remembering!'

PowerPointlessness

In the early 1990s, PowerPoint was heralded as a saviour for those presenting information. PowerPoint held the promise of making every presentation engaging and exciting. Gone were the overhead transparencies (and gone was my beloved pointer in the shape of a hand). Once we mastered the sound effects and the transition mode, our presentations with PowerPoint were going to be amazing. Sure, most people couldn't read what was on the slide but it made a really cool 'swoosh' sound, which just added to the excitement. And with hundreds of clip art images to insert, every slide looked amazing.

With this amazing technology, we could present without actually having to think about our messages and our audiences. Except, of course, we couldn't. The reality was quite different. PowerPoint sentenced us to presentation hell. As audience members, we were trapped in this slow, horrible death by PowerPoint and, as presenters, we were trapped in the unavoidable expectation of using it...and, sadly, in most companies we still are. I mentor many leaders on how they can be more engaging presenters and I often suggest not using PowerPoint—only to hear responses along the lines of 'I have to; it's expected and if I don't I will look unprepared'. So they reluctantly conform and give in to this weight of expectation. As Jean Paul Gaultier said, 'To conform is to give in'.

Peter Norvig, director of research at Google, states that 'PowerPoint doesn't kill meetings. People kill meetings. But using PowerPoint is like having a loaded AK-47 on the table: You can do very bad things with it.' PowerPoint is not the problem; the poor use of it is the problem. Having said that, the way PowerPoint is designed lends itself to a very linear structure. Professor Edward Tufte's essay 'The cognitive style of PowerPoint' explains two major problems with PowerPoint that influence how ineffective it is as a communication platform.

Tufte explains that PowerPoint is most often used as a guide for the presenter, rather than as an aid for the audience, and it causes ideas to be arranged in an unnecessarily deep hierarchy, which then means the audience needs to be taken through a very linear progression.

A friend once asked me for help with his PowerPoint slides. He knew I did a fair bit of presenting so assumed I would be a technical whiz at PowerPoint. However, although I told him I could help him out a bit because I had worked in the corporate world where PowerPoint was the expected medium, I also advised him I now very rarely used it. He was a bit shocked and said, 'But if you don't use PowerPoint, everyone is looking at you and not the slides'.

When I present, I actually want people to be looking at me and not being distracted by slides. What my friend highlighted was the fact that many presenters use PowerPoint as a crutch, to either deflect the attention off them or provide a guide for them so they don't forget their place.

That is why we see, to this day, slides with way too much text on them. Professor Tufte's research uncovered how PowerPoint was ineffectively used to brief senior NASA officials prior to the 2003 *Columbia* disaster, in which seven astronauts lost their lives after the space shuttle disintegrated during re-entry. The paper explores how vital information was buried in the PowerPoint presentation by the sheer amount of data on each slide.

Having heavily text-laden slides that your audience needs to read while you also talk them through the information is completely ineffective in taking in information.

Professor John Sweller from the University of New South Wales is well known for his work on cognitive load theory. Professor Sweller showed that the human brain processes information better if it is *either* in the written format or verbal. To get both versions of the same information simultaneously reduces the brain's ability to process the information. So asking a person to read off the slide as you are also talking reduces the effectiveness of your presentation. If you want people to read text, let them read it. Give them time to read it in silence and then perhaps ask some questions about it—such as, 'What stood out for you in that text? What do you think will have the biggest impact for us? What are you most concerned about when reading that?' According to Sweller, talking while also showing a diagram is fine, because the information is in a different form. But talking about the same words that are presented in the slide just puts too much load on the brain. Sweller sums up his theory by saying, 'The use of the PowerPoint presentation has been a disaster'.

This research really challenges the way most of us have been instructed to develop our PowerPoint presentations.

The current paradigm of capturing what you want to say in bullet points is just not working, and research is available to prove it. Of course, I don't really need to even cite the research — no doubt you've been in presentations where the presenters have talked through every bullet point on the slide. You know how boring and frustrating that is.

What we end up with is something called *PowerPointlessness* (a phrase coined by Barb Jenkins, who works at the South Australian Department of Education and Training). This covers 'the senseless use of PowerPoint to communicate with too many bells and whistles, animated transitions between slides and very little substance'.

Of course, creating the bells and whistles in a PowerPoint slide is the easy bit. Ensuring your content is relevant and communicable in an engaging and inspiring way is the hard bit. You need to focus less on the sizzle and more on the sausage. And remember the words of Edward Tufte, who said, 'If your words or images are not on point, making them dance in colour won't make them relevant'.

ENSURING YOUR CONTENT IS RELEVANT AND COMMUNICABLE IN AN ENGAGING AND INSPIRING WAY IS THE HARD BIT. YOU NEED TO FOCUS LESS ON THE *sizzle* AND MORE ON THE SAUSAGE.

The following sections discuss my top rules for creating presentations using PowerPoint (or Keynote).

Rule 1: Reduce your slides

Reduce both the content on your slides and the number of slides. People still put way too much content on their slides. I know of one organisation that had a minimum font size to try to address this, only to find their employees widened the margins of each slide.

My general rule for the ratio of PowerPoint slides to time is one slide for every three to five minutes. Always remember that less is more. If you're in doubt, try halving the number of slides you use. If you have 40 slides, make it 20; if you have 20, make it 10. Your audience does not need to see everything you are saying.

Rule 2: Make sure your slides are legible

Nothing is worse than showing a slide and saying, 'You probably can't read this, but...' I'm sure you've seen such a slide. The font used is tiny or the diagram has so many labels attached it makes no sense. Showing such a slide is insulting to your audience, and it makes you look lazy and like a poor presenter. Promise me if during a presentation you ever utter the words, 'You probably can't read this' you will add 'because I am a lazy presenter and I couldn't figure out a better way to communicate this to you'. Instead of having to make such an admission, think about using a handout instead, writing up key information on a whiteboard or replacing the information on the slide with your key point.

Rule 3: Remember a picture paints a thousand words

Every slide does not need to contain text. You can insert pictures, photos or simple diagrams. If you're using a story to convey a message, you could use an image that represents what you're saying. Just remember to keep it real—use your own photos rather than stock photos.

Once I was involved in a project that took nearly three years to complete. When I presented to the business about the completed project, I began by showing a photo of my daughter, who was two years old at the time. I knew full well that everyone was wondering why I was talking about my daughter and showing a picture of her. But one of the main points I wanted to get across from the start was how long and intensive the project had been. So I talked about my two-year-old daughter for about thirty seconds and then said, 'When we started this project, I was six weeks pregnant.'

Rule 4: Split your presentation

Not everyone will turn up on the day of your presentation, and so some people may miss out on information. To combat this, many presenters produce a PowerPoint pack, rich in text, that can be emailed out to those who didn't attend. Providing the information by email is a good idea but, if you decide to do this, don't think you need to include the text within the slide. Instead, convert the information to a document in Word and add text there, or put all the additional text into the notes pages of the PowerPoint presentation.

Remember that presentations are about what's right for the audience first, and then about you. The PowerPoint slides should only be used if they assist the audience in understanding and remembering your message—they shouldn't be used as prompts for you.

Prompts are always a good idea but have separate notes for that. Again, adding additional text may help you but it will have a detrimental effect on people understanding and remembering your message.

Before the presentation

Success depends upon previous preparation, and without such preparation there is sure to be failure.

—Confucius, Chinese philosopher

You should do certain things before your presentation. Some of these should be done well in advance, like days or weeks before your presentation, some the night before or morning of your presentation, and others literally just before you take the stage. The following sections take you through these preparations.

Well before your presentation

To make sure you're organised and calm on the day of your presentation, you can do some prep work days or weeks beforehand. Consider working through the following.

Check requirements

Nothing is more off-putting than when you walk into a room expecting one thing and finding another. To avoid any surprises, going through requirements well in advance of your presentation is definitely worthwhile.

For example, if you need any form of technology, make sure it is present. If you have a slide deck of any description, send it to the organiser in advance and also have a copy on a memory stick—both in the original version (such as Keynote or PowerPoint) and also exported as a PDF. You may be using Keynote only to find that the venue does not support Mac products. Saving your presentation as a PDF averts this crisis.

Besides checking your requirements can be met, it is also a good idea to check details such as the following:

- What time will you be presenting?
- How many people will be there?
- What will the previous speaker be talking about?
- Will drinks or food be served while you are speaking?

On most occasions, if you get an answer to one of the preceding questions that's not ideal, you won't be able to do anything to change it—but you will at least minimise surprises on the day.

It is also a good idea to check the dress code. You need to dress to impress, but also dress for the situation. Sometimes that will require you suiting up, other times going more casual. My general rule is always go one standard higher than the dress code.

You can also use this as an opportunity to create and display a signature personal style that is relevant to who you are. I try to wear a splash of orange whenever I present because it is my branding colour, but you could go with anything that works for you. Creating your own signature style is a good way to be remembered.

CREATING YOUR OWN SIGNATURE STYLE IS A GOOD WAY TO BE *remembered*.

Request a lapel

I have never been a fan of the lectern, mainly because it places an unnecessary barrier between you and your audience and I think it is a contributing factor to stopping you from presenting the real you on stage.[2]

I was not surprised, then, to find that the word 'lectern' ultimately comes from the Latin word 'legere', which means 'to read'. General definitions refer to the lectern as 'a reading desk with a slanted top used to hold a sacred text from which passages are read in a religious service; a stand that serves as a support for the notes or books of a speaker'.

In fact, its first recorded use was in religious ceremonies where it was used as a place for the speaker to stand while presenting religious teaching during a church service. The sloping top of the lectern provided a convenient place for the speaker's scrolls, script or book, typically the Bible.

So no doubt many people associate lecterns with their more formal origins. If possible, break away from this formality and always get out from behind the lectern. Using a podium or lectern cuts off 50-plus per cent of most people's bodies, which is why the lectern is a physical barrier between you and your audience, preventing you from truly connecting. If you're on the short side, your audience may only see a head, part of your upper torso and your arms poking out the side.

When behind a lectern, you can also inadvertently do things that have a negative impact. You may find yourself leaning on it or gripping the sides, especially when nervous. Many speakers refer to their notes too often because they are literally right under their nose, not because they need to. This often means the presenter starts reading, which can have the complete opposite effect of presenting the real you on stage and should be avoided at all times.

---

[2] It may also be due to my earliest memories of going to Sunday church and having the priest deliver sermons on how I should live.

So I highly recommend staying away from using a lectern if at all possible. If you must speak from one, don't hide behind it and don't grip it; make lots of eye contact and use large gestures that your audience can see.

The other option, of course, is to use a lapel microphone. You can attach this to your clothing so your hands are free and you are free to move out from behind the lectern. A handheld microphone also allows you this freedom but, if you have a choice, go with the lapel microphone over the handheld microphone. The main problem with the handheld microphone is that you have to hold it all the way through your presentation, which means you only have one arm to make hand gestures and you may also cause variance in sound quality as you move the microphone too close or too far away from your mouth.

Don't assume that a lapel microphone will be available on the day. Always enquire well in advance of your presentation.

A lapel mic consists of the battery component and the microphone, and both need to be secured to separate pieces of appropriate clothing. So what you wear needs careful consideration, especially if you are a female as the options beyond suit and shirt increase.

The battery compartment of the lapel mic can be a bit heavy, so it needs to be clipped to something that can support this weight, such as a sturdy leather belt.

Check what your bio says about you

As a professional speaker, I am often asked to provide a short bio so the MC of the event can introduce me, and perhaps so the organisers of the event can circulate this bio beforehand. Even if the conference organisers don't ask for this bio I provide it anyway, because I don't want my introduction to be left to chance. Losing control of what people say about you when they introduce you isn't a great start. Too often I have seen people introduced by the MC reading out a short version of their CV, listing previous jobs and experience. This can result in the audience being bored with that person before they even take the stage.

Your presentation bio is an opportunity for you to communicate real information about you that people would not ordinarily hear. It's a chance to build credibility, particularly on the topic you are about to talk about. It's an opportunity to demonstrate a value you have and it is a chance to be more real. And you don't even have to do anything too radical to stand out.

Your bio should be a combination of professional and personal achievements. It should include your past and your present and it should articulate your passion. Finally, it should be short and tailored for what is relevant to your audience.

My approach is to 'Five P' your bio, which means you should include information that covers professional, personal, past and present areas of your life. At the centre of everything should be your passion.

Following are some suggestions and examples you could include for each of your 5Ps. You don't need to include all of these in your bio because it would become too long. Just pick the ones that are the most relevant and remember this is all about being less boring and more real.

Past professional aspects could include:

- work history
- industry experience
- qualifications
- clients you have worked with
- locations you have worked in
- books you have authored.

Your present professional information could cover:

- current title
- current projects or work
- current clients
- future exciting opportunities.

Past personal aspects could be:

- past sporting achievements—for example, running a marathon
- past experiences you are proud of (even if these are a bit quirky)—runner-up in your Grade 2 spelling bee competition
- relevant family history—one leader I knew introduced himself by saying he was calm because he grew up in a house with seven sisters, three brothers and one bathroom.

Present personal areas could include:

- current hobbies or sport—for example, currently training for a half marathon
- future exciting opportunities such as holidays or significant family occasions—your son's wedding, the birth of your child or grandchild, your daughter's 21st birthday.

Your passion can be stated explicitly in your bio or implied. Your passion ideally should be related to helping your audience. For example, 'I am passionate about helping leaders be the most inspiring leaders they can be' or 'I am obsessed about providing the best service to our customers'.

Prioritise practice

Being a real presenter does not mean you don't practise.

It's easy to say practise, practise, practise but the reality is that most of us just don't and that is due to a whole lot of reasons. Within my work with leaders (especially in the corporate world) I come across a variety reasons that stop them from practising, but by the far the most common is 'time'.

Time is obviously a key factor that will determine how much we practise but the other factor is, or at least should be, familiarity of content. These will determine how much and what we practise before any presentation.

Time

Time is the biggest excuse I hear for not practising but it's not necessarily the real reason. Granted, as a leader you are often asked to give a presentation with very little notice but most of the time you at least get some notice. That may only be a few days or a few hours but there is normally enough notice to do some practice.

Content

How well you know the content will also determine how much time you need to practise. If you have presented the same content on numerous times, you probably need to do very little practice — although you should always check that the content and the way it is delivered is still appropriate for this exact audience. This may be as simple as running through what examples or stories you share to get your point across, and choosing the most appropriate ones for the audience you are about to present to.

Practice quadrant model

To determine how much practice time may be required, I came up with the practice quadrant model. This title is pretty dry, so after many variations I decided to call it the practical practise practice. A bit of a mouthful, yes, but the idea is that you should get into the practice of practising practically. The model is shown in the following illustration.

As you can see from the model, if the content is new and you have a lot of time, you should be aiming to practise ALL STUFF. What I mean by this is practise a lot and make sure you do a complete run-through of your presentation.

If you don't have a lot of time but the content is mostly new, just practise the NEW STUFF. So focus on the content that you are not overly familiar with and make sure you get your head around this new content. What is riding on the presentation can also affect what you choose to focus on.

If the content is familiar and you have time on your side, just practise the KEY STUFF—that is, the opening and closing, and the part that delivers your key message. If using a story, include practising the story in your key stuff. When practising only on key stuff and new stuff, you don't need to do a full run-through.

If, on the other hand, the content is familiar and you have little time, practise STUFF ALL. This is perhaps the only time I would say it is absolutely okay not to practise and still be able to do a good job. Any practice you do here is a bonus.

Some tips for practice

The power of practice can't be underestimated, and you should try to practise aloud, not just in your head. Practising aloud is a real test for 'Is this the real you?' You will hear what words are not sounding right for you. Try to use language you would normally use because this is about real talk and presenting the real you on stage.

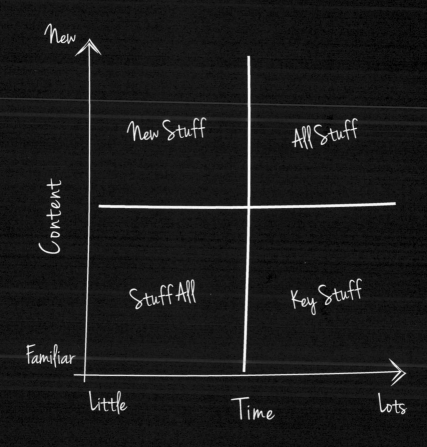

Here are some further tips:

- Practise alone in the car, in the shower, or when you are going for a run or a walk.

- Practise by recording yourself on your phone and listening back to it.[3]

- Make sure you practise in front of someone, even if this is your partner at home. Presenting to just one other person makes your presentation come alive — there is now a dynamic, and you might speed up or slow down.

- Practise, practise and then practise some more.

The final tip, and perhaps the most important, is find a method that works for you. Some people suggest practising in front of a mirror. Personally I hate this because I look at myself and start to become all self-conscious about minor things. I end up focusing on me as opposed to my message or potential audience.

Find a way that works for you and go for it.

Just before your presentation

Even with the best laid plans, you still have a few points you can check off right before presenting. They are covered here.

Know your routine

Most Olympic athletes have a routine they religiously perform before each event. Sport psychologists call this 'mindfulness' or 'process focusing'. It's helpful because it focuses the mind on the present moment and so distracts the brain from racing ahead.

---

[3]Don't worry — most people hate their recorded voice.

During the 2004 Athens Olympics, for example, Australian swim coach Shannon Rollason instructed swimmer Jodie Henry to have a routine for the twenty minutes preceding each race. Swimmers have this amount of time between leaving the change rooms and finally getting on the blocks to race, and it's enough time for nerves and doubts to build. On leaving the change room, Shannon told Jodie she was to speak to someone in the marshalling area; then she was to find the Australian team and wave to them. Next, she had to seek out her parents in the audience and give them a wave. When she was introduced she had to wave and then, and only then, was she to take off her tracksuit and put her cap on. Henry won three Olympic gold medals in the 2004 games using this pre-match routine. Granted, the fact that she could swim faster than anyone else in the pool probably contributed more to her wins than her routine, but in the past her nerves had prevented her from proving this. Having a routine that works for you can certainly help.

The routine that works for you might be as simple as doing a final practice in your head, or listening to a particular song that relaxes you or fires you up.

Visualise success

In an experiment conducted by Australian psychologist Alan Richardson, a group of basketball players was split into three smaller groups. One group was told to practise their free-throw technique for 20 minutes every day. The next group was told to spend 20 minutes every day visualising, but not practising, free throws. The last group was not allowed to either practise or visualise their free throws. At the end of the experiment period, the group who had done nothing remained as they were, but both the other groups showed similar degrees of improvement. The people who only visualised playing basketball were able to perform almost as well as the ones who had actually practised. How can that be so?

145

Well, the people practising missed some shots. Each time they missed they had, in effect, practised how to miss. The people who were visualising hit every basket, so they were building up the feelings and memory of how to be successful.

Visualisation is an incredibly powerful and simple way of speeding up the improvement process by fooling the mind into believing that you have already done something before you have. Of course, this in and of itself will not turn you into an NBA star, or an inspiring presenter. You actually have to practise as well, but it will help you succeed more quickly.

During the 1996 Atlanta Olympics, for example, the Australian men's rowing team (who were known as the 'Oarsome Foursome') had only just scraped into the final. Against all odds, they went on to win gold in the event. They put this down to sport psychologist Jeff Bond, who had worked with them on positive visualisation in the lead-up to Atlanta. They practised the event over and over in their heads—warming up, paddling and finishing the race. Apparently, on the day it went exactly as they had visualised.

You too can use the same technique. In the week leading up to your presentation, picture yourself walking on stage, engaging your audience at the start, going through your key messages, finishing with a lot of applause as you leave the stage and getting all the great feedback afterwards.

Visualising success works because the brain cannot distinguish between reality and imagination. After you have visualised something like this in detail, when you actually stand up to present, your mind feels it's done this before. The more you visualise success, the more you'll trick your mind into thinking it is real.

I must admit I was a bit sceptical of this approach but I have grown to use it and can now say it works. At a minimum, it helps reduce the nerves and anxiety.

Use power posing

Amy Cuddy is a Harvard Business School professor[4] who gave a TED talk that has received more than 21 million views to date.[5] Cuddy's research links our body language to our hormone levels, our feelings and our behaviour. Her research shows that even faking powerful body postures that convey competence and power can change our testosterone (dominance) and cortisol (stress) levels. Cuddy calls this 'power posing' and it can be effective after faking it for only a couple of minutes. With this increase in testosterone and cortisol levels, we increase our appetite for risk and have greater ability to cope well in stressful situations.

IF YOU ACT *powerfully*, YOU WILL BEGIN TO THINK POWERFULLY, AND WHEN PEOPLE FEEL POWERFUL, THEY BECOME MORE *present*.

Cuddy believes that our body language can shape who we are, and that the non-verbal gestures we make can govern what other people think and feel about us. Non-verbals can even govern the way we think and feel about ourselves.

If you act powerfully, you will begin to think powerfully, and when people feel powerful, they become more present. They become better connected with their own thoughts and feelings, which can help them to better connect with the thoughts and feelings of others. This can allow a presenter to significantly increase their chances of connecting, engaging and captivating an audience.

---

[4] Just to show I do mention Harvard when it has nothing to do with me.
[5] To view, search online for 'Amy Cuddy body language'.

During the presentation

If you have prepared like a professional, you have done a lot of hard work leading up to your presentation. During your presentation you should still be mindful of certain things. The following pages outline a few aspects you need to focus on as you present.

Put the audience first

You need to put your audience's needs ahead of yours. Once I was asked to deliver a keynote presentation as part of an internal leadership conference. I was the last speaker of the day. I had to fly to the event so I arrived a few hours early and decided to sit in on earlier presentations so I could weave any themes or messages into my presentation.

It was a glorious spring day in Sydney. The conference room was directly on the water with spectacular views of the Sydney Harbour Bridge. And the best bit was that the conference rooms had floor-to-ceiling glass walls so you could make the most of this amazing view.

However, every speaker who presented was using PowerPoint, so the blockout blinds had to be drawn to avoid the sun glare making it difficult for the audience to see the screen.

During the afternoon tea-break, I was getting my lapel microphone attached and tested along with the other speaker who was on just before me. Someone asked him about his presentation and he said he was not using PowerPoint. I told him I only had provided PowerPoint slides because the organisers had insisted, and I would also be happy to not use them because it would allow the blockout blinds to be raised and the view to be appreciated.

Someone suggested that people may look at the view instead of listening to me. I was happy to take that risk and, at one stage, that is exactly what happened. I was talking away and noticed that quite a lot of eyes were looking past me and out the window. I stopped and turned around to see a large tall ship, with all sails drawn, sailing past directly under the harbour bridge. It was an impressive sight that I commented on. I waited the twenty seconds or so it took to sail by and then continued.

It is easy for ego to come into play here and tell yourself, 'Everyone should be listening to me', but it's not about you. It's about them. Keep it real and put your audience first.

Be flexible

Life is never perfect, so things are often going to go wrong. Your presentation time may be cut, the technology may fail, you may be asked an unexpected curly question or you may be interrupted by an audience member who informs you that your topic was just covered by another speaker.

Being flexible in your approach to your content and context will allow you to recover from these setbacks.

A presenter I know, Jane, once had a problem with her slides—they kept randomly moving forwards and backwards, and the remote she was using did not seem to be controlling them. After repeatedly asking the support crew to revert back to the slide she wanted, she decided to ditch them all together and had the support crew turn the system off. Jane found out later that the remotes had been switched between rooms and the presenter in the next room was controlling the flow of her slides.

When things go wrong, the audience has the opportunity to see the real you. How you respond can be critical. Not that you would want something wrong to happen but, if it does, it can create an amazing opportunity for the real you to shine.

It's showtime!

If you want to be engaging and inspiring, you have to treat every presentation like opening night. Even if it is a presentation you have done many times, you need to understand that this is opening night for your audience.

I was once told a story from an interview with Bruce Springsteen. The interviewer asked him how he kept up his motivation to deliver live performances, night after night, after 30 years in the industry. Springsteen replied, 'It was when I realised that, while for me, every night is a 'Bruce Springsteen concert night' there are thousands of people in the audience who have spent their money to see a Bruce Springsteen concert maybe for the first and only time in their lives. They may only come to one Bruce Springsteen concert in their life and I want to give them the best ever Bruce Springsteen experience. And that's what keeps me going night after night.'

So think like Springsteen next time you are about to step on stage and give your audience your own version of a first Springsteen concert (you probably don't need to belt out 'Born to Run'...although that would be unusual).

Use your pace

Nothing is more tedious than listening to a presenter stuck on one speed—whether that pace is slow, or super-fast. It comes across as fake or over-rehearsed...a long way from 'real'. A singular pace can often happen when people read from a script.

Getting your pace right is important, but that also means that you vary your pace at particular points. This helps keep and sustain your audience's attention and stops you developing a monotone.

It's natural that your audience's attention will vary throughout your presentation. Seldom is anyone going

IT'S SHOWTIME!

- Put your audience first
- Be flexible
- Use your pace
- Use your space

to be hanging on every word you say. The harsh reality is you will lose your audience at different points as they zone out—perhaps to think about what's for dinner or if they hung out the washing. So you should give them the opportunity to refocus on you. Varying your pace is an underused technique that helps you do exactly that.

When you are presenting an important point, slow down your normal pace by about 10 per cent—that is, look at your baseline pace and slow it down by 10 per cent. Speaking slowly gives you a sense of authority. Just be careful not to do this too much—otherwise, it will have the opposite effect and you'll come across as patronising, like you're telling a child a bedtime story. Slow down slightly at particular points to increase your presence and impact.

Pausing in between words is also a sure-fire way to have a big impact. This kind of technique signals the importance of what you're saying. Recently I ran a group of leaders through an exercise focusing on this. Without telling them what I was doing I said, 'What I am about to share with you is really important'. I then remained silently present. I did not say a word for about ten seconds, but maintained eye contact the whole way. Then I asked them, 'What just happened?' They responded along the lines of, 'I just can't wait to hear what you are about to say' and 'You had me totally intrigued and had my full attention'.

Just as slowing down and pausing can work to keep or grab an audience's attention, so too can speeding up your pace. If you are sharing an exciting, high-energy point or even a story with lots of action in it, you should speed up what you are saying by at least 10 to 15 per cent. Speeding up recreates the energy and excitement of the story. It's natural to talk fast when we're excited or eager and the aim here is to mimic natural conversational patterns.

Use your space

All the world's a stage.

—William Shakespeare, English playwright

When you are presenting, all your world at that moment is the stage, so use it. Now, of course, every stage will be different—some will be longer, some wider, and they will be different shapes or heights. Regardless of what the stage looks like, make it work for you and take control of it.

You have a lapel microphone on (hopefully) so you are not anchored to the lectern. Get out there and use the stage—but make sure you meander with purpose.

Walking around on stage does a couple of things for you:

- It can create interest and energy.

- It can make you look more confident and feel more confident.

Here are some ways you can meander around the stage with purpose:

- The power position on the stage is front and centre. Use this space to both open and close your presentation and to get across your key messages.

- Move to the front of the stage when you want to get closer to your audience and when you feel you need to make a connection or emphasise a point. When I share a personal story, for example, I always move closer to the front of the stage.

- Move from left to right on the stage to emphasise the past, present and future.

And here are a few further things to consider:

- Make sure you do not walk out of the lighted area. Your audience always needs to see you.

- If there are obstacles in the room (such as columns that block some audience members' view), avoid these spots so the audience can see you most of the time.

- During the sound check, identify any no-go zones where you lose sound or trigger that annoying, ear-piercing screech from microphone interference.

After the presentation

So you may think that as soon as you walk off the stage, your job is done. But it is not. Just as you have things to consider before and during your presentation, you also have things to consider after your presentation.

Thank people

I am not talking about thanking the audience at the end of your speech. That is a given. However, one thing to note is that you should try not to do so with a 'Thank you for listening'. I try to end with something along the lines of 'It's been a pleasure being with you' or 'Thanks for your energy and interaction; I hope you enjoy the rest of the conference'.

Also showing gratitude to the people who asked you to speak is an important element of presenting. Take the opportunity to be grateful to the people in the audience who came to see you as well as the organisers who invited you to speak.

Small gestures like this can make such a big difference. If you're not already in the habit of thanking people, it may be a good habit to adopt. It doesn't matter whether you've just given a keynote speech, a presentation that you are being paid handsomely for, pro-bono work or a presentation at your team's sales conference—give thanks, because you've been given an opportunity that you should be thankful for.

Seek feedback and reflect

So how did you go? Do a quick evaluation of what worked and what didn't. What should you do more of? What could you do better? I often blog about things as a way to reflect and also to share what I learnt from an experience.

You could use a variety of feedback and reflective models, but I just ask myself three simple questions:

1 What did I do well? What seemed to work for the audience?

2 What didn't work that I would not use again?

3 What could I do differently or better next time?

Also reflect on your presentation through the lens of 'How real did this feel?' When did you feel you were being real? When did everything seem to flow? Try to do more of that and your presentations will feel more real—and I can guarantee you, when that happens you start to enjoy them more.

Apart from self-reflection, seeking out feedback from others is also a good idea. You could ask a trusted adviser in the audience how it went. Were people engaged? Sometimes the questions, or lack of questions, after you have presented is also an indicator.

I recall I once went to an appalling breakfast presentation and when the organisers asked for questions at the end, there were none. This is an indication; this is feedback for you as the presenter. Some presenters also record their presentations so they can watch or listen to them afterwards, and pick up the bits that worked and those they could improve on.

It does not matter how you reflect, just make sure you do.

Strive

Besides seeking feedback and reflecting after each presentation, you can do a couple of other things as you strive to be a better presenter:

- *Observe other speakers*—when you're in the audience and listening to an inspiring presenter, observe what they're doing and be curious about that. What are they doing that makes it such a great presentation? How do they use the stage? When are they sharing their stories? How are they interacting with the audience? Watch some TED talks online and do the same. I encourage you to use your two eyes and ears when watching presenters. One to actually take in what you are hearing and seeing but the other to observe what is happening and what tools are being used.

- *Get a mentor*—find a mentor to help you develop your content, your style and your confidence. Leaders have coaches for all sorts of things and it's worthwhile considering a mentor to help with your presenting.

Chapter 6

Presenting the real you online

Chapter 5 focused on the topic of presenting the real you, and while on this topic it is worth dedicating a chapter to presenting the real you online. In this digital age, you cannot escape your online presence and it is just as important to keep it real online as it is in person. From your website (if you have one) to your LinkedIn profile, your online presence can have an effect on how others see you.

How you appear online is often the first impression people get of you — most people will do an online search on you before meeting with you — so it's worthwhile investing time and energy into making your online presence a real representation of you.

HOW YOU APPEAR ONLINE IS OFTEN THE FIRST *impression* PEOPLE GET OF YOU.

While Facebook is a hugely popular social media platform, the platform for businesspeople is LinkedIn. LinkedIn has been around longer than Facebook and is one of the most effective social media sites for professionals. Your LinkedIn page is also likely to be the main online platform you can influence when looking to ensure what people see online is the real you. If you have one, your website is another strong tool for representing you, so I cover this area briefly at the end of the chapter.

Taking advantage of LinkedIn

In this section, I outline five ways to help make your LinkedIn profile more engaging and real.

Remember first impressions count

You wouldn't go to a networking event with a mask on and, equally, you shouldn't hide your face on your LinkedIn profile. You should include a photo.

Having a clear, professional photo on your profile will allow you to have more impact and credibility. Having a photo that genuinely reflects the real you and what you do is also important.

Look at your headline and summary

Don't think that your headline automatically needs to be your positional title. Could you use something from your bio as your tagline? Perhaps you could highlight your passion or use a combination of your passion and your title, such as: 'Head of Customer Service and passionate about making a difference'.

The summary area is also an important one to look at. Many people don't provide a summary or simply use this feature to capture their work experience. However,

LinkedIn provides a specific section where you can capture work experience and skills, so you don't need to duplicate the information here.

Look back at the work you did when creating your bio for presentations (focusing on your 5Ps—refer to chapter 5). Think about whether you could use your bio as your LinkedIn summary or a revised version of that.

One last point—the jury seems to be out on whether the summary should be written in first person or not. However, I am a fan of using the first person because I just think it seems more real.

Actively contribute

Don't be a bystander with LinkedIn. If you come across an article you find valuable and that you think others in your network will also find of value, share it.

If you have an insight into an article, make a comment.

If you like a comment, 'like' it.

The only time you can contribute to LinkedIn is when you are sharing your messages, and sharing the messages of others. Doing so will help build your reputation as an expert in your field, but also give people a clearer idea of your passions and opinions.

Publish posts that highlight your passions

After reading through chapter 2, you should have a clearer idea on what your chimes are, what you believe in and what you stand for. LinkedIn and other social media sites are a way to start communicating these chimes and beliefs, through the posts or comments you add.

Either write your own posts and publish them on LinkedIn or share others' posts with a comment on why you shared them.

Connect well

You can usually find a smarter way to do most things in life, and connecting on LinkedIn is no exception. When you want to connect with someone, don't just send them a standard request, Instead, always try to include a personal note on why you want to connect with them.

I also find that I more readily accept requests to connect with people when they add a personal note, such as 'I saw you speak recently and would like to connect', or 'I just read your book and would like to connect'.

Once I received the following LinkedIn request to connect from someone in the UK:

> Hi
>
> We have not done business together but I am on your mailing list and enjoyed the last one. I hope you accept my invitation to connect here on LinkedIn.
>
> Kind regards

I think the way this person reached out to connect was polite and professional—and just common sense. These attributes are sometimes forgotten in the world of social media.

Finally, keep your profile up to date. As you change, make sure your profile reflects that. Keep it current and keep it relevant—but, most importantly, keep it real.

Making your website work for you

While a full rundown of website design is beyond the scope of this book, I can give you a few pointers when it comes to its content, and making sure you still show the real you.

When it comes to your own website (if you have one), you may feel that the site needs to be void of any of your own personality. Many leaders feel like this. However, just as we can attempt to be 'real' in person, we can also take that same philosophy to our website.

If we are prepared to show our passions, values and beliefs in person, we should aim for the same courage on our website.

One perfect place to show this is in the 'about' section. Perhaps, for example, you could share a personal story in this section that shows your passion or values. For example, in mine I share the following story.

When I left school I applied for a job as computer operator. I was pretty rapt to get an interview and I thought I performed well in it. The following weekend, I saw the job advertised again and can recall saying to Mum, 'Obviously I did not get the job'. She suggested I apply for it again. So after thinking, Yeah, right, how lame would that be? I actually did apply for it again, writing a much stronger letter. I was asked in for a second interview, where the manager said to me, 'Your second letter was lot stronger; why did you apply for the job again?' I told him it was because I really wanted the job and I really knew I could do it (I may have left out the bit about my Mum telling me to). I was offered the job on the spot.

Fast-forward to about 17 years later. It was 4 am and my young daughter was screaming for her bottle. As my husband was heating up her bottle, he said to her, 'Hang on the bottle's coming soon; good things come to those that wait'. I remember snapping at him with, 'Don't you ever say that to our daughter again. It's a stupid saying. Good things don't come to those who wait; good things come to those who get out there and do something about it, and when they fail they don't give up they try something different.'

At this point, I think he suggested that perhaps I should go back to bed and he would do that feed.

So, yes, in my first-time mother, sleep-deprived state that was obviously an unjustified overreaction but it is something I truly believe. People who know me well know that one of my all-time favourite quotes is 'If you always do what you have always done, you will always get what you have always got'.

I am passionate about working with people to give them the clarity, confidence and capability to achieve their authentic potential, to be the most inspiring leader they can be and to make the difference they were born to make.

Don't be afraid to inject some of the real you into your website.

CONCLUSION

In pursuit of knowledge, every day something is acquired; in pursuit of wisdom, every day something is dropped.

—Lao Tzu, Chinese philosopher

I love the above quote because it highlights the importance of stopping just as much as starting. We spend our professional careers and, in fact, our lives acquiring new skills that we need to practise and take onboard. If it seems like an endless journey of learning new knowledge, that's because it is. What this quote from Lao Tzu highlights, however, is it is just as critical to stop doing things. This applies to our professional lives and our personal lives. If you decide to start doing sit-ups to get rid of that muffin top but continue to eat muffins, nothing is likely to change.

I hope this book has provided some knowledge and tips that you can apply to your leadership, and given you some insights that will result in you doing something differently.

The change you make may be as simple as not using PowerPoint at your next presentation or sharing a personal story during your presentation. It may involve taking a stand for something at work or saying 'no' to something. Regardless how big or small the change is, I encourage you to make the change.

A final word

Can you indulge me one more time and allow me to share a final experience from my time at Harvard?

While at Harvard, one of the concepts we explored was the 'frontier of competence' and how you have to push yourself through this frontier for personal growth to occur. It would be fair to say that I discovered my frontier of competence several times in the classrooms of Harvard. It's that edge you're taken to when you realise you still have so much to learn and you have to take the leap to keep learning. It's that moment when you go from unconscious incompetence to conscious incompetence. It's a scary and humbling place to be but I think we owe it to ourselves to keep finding our frontier of competence and pushing through it.

In your various roles—as leader, teacher, coach and perhaps parent—you must work with the people you care for to safely take them to their frontier of competence and, when the time is right, help them push through it.

The confronting aspect of the frontier of competence is that the cycle never ends. I have always likened professional development in leadership to painting the Sydney Harbour Bridge—it is such a massive task that, as soon as you finish it, you have to start again. So, in reality, you never finish.

Three days after I had finished the Harvard program and was still processing what I learned, I took my very first walk across the Brooklyn Bridge in New York. As I crossed,

I saw a sole worker painting the bridge with a hand roller. Considering the Brooklyn Bridge is one of the longest suspension bridges in the world, that is a lot of steel cable to paint with a hand roller.

Again, the professional and personal development cycle is never-ending—just at the point when you think you are almost done, it will be time to start again...just like painting the Brooklyn Bridge or the Sydney Harbour Bridge.

So I encourage you to make a start, one cable at a time. Dig deep to find out what you really believe in, what your true north is, what your chimes are and what your purpose is. Have the confidence to bring your whole self to your leadership. Have the courage to show emotion and vulnerability at work. Keep it real and say it as it is. Get out there and engage and inspire a whole generation of people eager to make a difference.

Be real and ignite yourself, and ignite the people you lead.

Stay connected

I would love to hear from you and hear what you thought about this book. You can stay connected and get in touch via any of the following:

- LinkedIn @ GabrielleDolan
- Twitter @ GabrielleDolan1
- website @ www.gabrielledolan.com
- email @ gabrielle@gabrielledolan.com

INDEX

MORE PRAISE FOR
GABRIELLE DOLAN

Elegant in its practicality, *Ignite* will challenge your ideas about leadership and set you on a path to achieving greater results in your organisation today. Gabrielle offers simple and straightforward advice on how to become a more 'real you' while exercising leadership in an increasingly complex world. Her reflections provide valuable leadership insights and a fresh outlook on communication.

—Bonnie Houston, Director of Organizational Development at National Oilwell Varco

Gabrielle keeps it 'real' throughout *Ignite*, which is both inspiring and practical for those who are already leaders and those who aspire to be. *Ignite* is as engaging a read as Gabrielle is in person. In answer to 'Is it worth the trip?' the answer in relation to *Ignite* is 'Yes'!

—Stephen Purcell, CEO at PPB Advisory

Gabrielle Dolan's crisp voice shines through the pages of *Ignite*. This book offers a refreshing walk through the landscape of leadership literature. It is rich in ideas and also provides nuts and bolts of how and when to use storytelling effectively. *Ignite* will change the way I teach and manage across generations.

—Aviva Luz Argote, Lecturer Tufts University; Associate, Breakthrough Collaboration

As our world becomes increasingly 'virtual', it is refreshing to read real stories about real people written by a real leader offering outstanding advice. Well done Gabrielle.

—Jac Phillips, Head of Brand and Marketing, Bank of Melbourne

I love all celebrations of difference, and you will find that and more in Gabrielle Dolan's new book, *Ignite*. Discover, as I did, all that is different and special about yourself as a leader and supercharge your influence. Gabrielle shares her insights in a fast-paced, funny and practical read. What's more, Gabrielle's personality shines from every page, providing us with inspiration and courage to take her advice. A rare book.

—Kath Walters, content marketing and media relations expert

A great how-to guide about self-awareness and authenticity, for leaders at all levels. A practical guide to understanding yourself and leading with confidence and courage in an increasingly challenging and changing environment. *Ignite* uses real language and offers practical help for leaders to act with clarity and conviction.

—Paul Stratford, General Manager—Talent Development and Performance, Telstra

In the world of fake smiles and handshakes, being real is the only way to engage and inspire people. That is the message Gabrielle Dolan points out throughout this excellent book filled with real stories and advice. Unlike other leadership literature, this book offers a valuable and practical framework for every leader who wants to improve on their storytelling and presenting skills. *Ignite* is a must-read for everyone engaged in the field of leadership.

—Davor Filipovic, Assistant Professor at University of Zagreb, Faculty of Economics and Business

Ignite is packed full of wisdom, insights and techniques for leaders who are serious about engaging and inspiring their people...and courageous enough to bring all of themselves to their work.

—Peter Cook, partner at Thought Leaders Global, author, keynote speaker, mentor

The insights Gabrielle Dolan has cultivated through her leadership journey and careful research part the mists of leadership to provide an absorbing treatise that is also, simply, a great read. This is a book that I will keep nearby and continue to reference, and distribute widely to my team and colleagues. In *Ignite*, Dolan speaks to the reader with the wit and frankness those who know her would recognise and appreciate, revealing her very own authentic self. Her mastery of the art of storytelling is evident, but that's another story (*Hooked*, to be precise!).

—Natalie Mina, Corporate Strategy Program Director; Global IT, consulting and outsourcing organisation

Gabrielle's book inspires us to go beyond the surface and get to the bottom of what is real and what truly moves people. Leadership is all about inspiring and harnessing energy, and Gabrielle offers the keys for successful leadership. To tap into that energy, relationships between individuals, teams and across the organisation have to ignite the whole person: brain, heart and gut. Gabrielle also shows how to engage the next generation to ignite their potential, something everyone in Human Resources will want to achieve. I recommend this book, so you can take your leadership to the next level in a powerful way.

**—Monica Howden, Senior HR Specialist
ASVITO Consulting**

What I love about Gabrielle Dolan is her no-nonsense, cut to the chase attitude and this is what I also love about *Ignite*. She's the real deal, as are her messages. The book is filled with powerful methods that teach leaders to develop in every way.

**—Christina Guidotti, speaker, author, mentor,
partner at Thought Leaders Global**

Thank you for taking the time to read this book and I truly hope it was of some value.

If you like what you read here you may be interested in my regular blog posts. They are insightful and witty, with a sprinkling of genius. Granted I may be a tad biased but others do find them of value. You can subscribe at: www.gabrielledolan.com.

The greatest compliment you can give an author if you loved their book is to write a fabulous online review at any online store. So if you feel inclined to do that I would truly appreciate it.

Feel free to reach out if you think I could add value to your company by working with your leaders on real leadership, storytelling or thought leadership. I speak, consult and train in these areas.

To find out more head to www.gabrielledolan.com or send me an email at info@gabrielledolan.com.

Until next time.

Gabrielle

Connect
with WILEY ▶▶▶

WILEY — Browse and purchase the full range of Wiley publications on our official website.

www.wiley.com

 Check out the Wiley blog for news, articles and information from Wiley and our authors.

www.wileybizaus.com

 Join the conversation on Twitter and keep up to date on the latest news and events in business.

@WileyBizAus

 Sign up for Wiley newsletters to learn about our latest publications, upcoming events and conferences, and discounts available to our customers.

www.wiley.com/email

 Wiley titles are also produced in e-book formats. Available from all good retailers.

WILEY

Learn more with practical advice from our experts

Hooked
*Gabrielle Dolan
and Yamini Naidu*

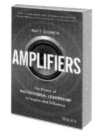

Amplifiers
Matt Church

Brave
Margie Warrell

**Doing Good by
Doing Good**
Peter Baines

The Game Changer
Jason Fox

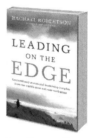

**Leading on the
Edge**
Rachael Robertson

From Me to We
Janine Garner

**The New Rules of
Management**
Peter Cook

**Selfish, Scared
and Stupid**
*Dan Gregory and
Kieran Flanagan*

Available in print and e-book formats

WILEY